The *Friendship Book*

of Francis Gay

A THOUGHT
FOR EACH DAY
IN 2011

D. C. THOMSON & CO., LTD.
London Glasgow Manchester Dundee

> *"We are each of us angels with only one wing,*
> *And we can fly only by embracing each other."*
>
> *Luciano de Crescenzo.*

January

SAYING goodbye to an old year and welcoming in a new one isn't always easy. What lies ahead of us might seem rather overwhelming, and what's behind us might still linger on leaving feelings of confusion, uncertainty, even resentment.

We have this need to see the whole picture, to understand everything. Well, we can't, but that's not up to us.

Step forward positively, trusting that everything is seen and understood. Greet the New Year with the words of Dag Hammarskjold: "For all that has been, thanks. For all that will be, yes."

JESUS once spoke of three men who were each given a sum of money to take care of by their master. One buried his, while the others used theirs to increase what they'd already been given.

Whether you're an artist, a great cook, or someone who makes the ideal friend, we all have God-given talents of a different sort, and it's up to us how we develop them. We can stay the way we are, or we can get to work and make the very best of our skills, using them to help other people.

"God's gift to us is who we are, and our gift to God is who we become." Let's use the gifts we've been given, and give something back.

Monday — **January 3**

A TRAVELLER once asked a wise man sitting at the city walls what the people inside were like.

"What are the people like in the city you come from?" replied the wise man. The stranger then pondered a moment.

"They're generous and kind, they're patient and good folk," he said.

"Well, that's how you'll find them here," the wise man said.

A few days later another traveller came to the city and asked the wise man the same question. "What are the people like in the city you come from?" the wise man wanted to know. Again there was some hesitation.

"The people are fairly mean," he said. "They're a grumpy lot and pretty miserable."

"Well," said the wise man, "that's just how you'll find people here."

Tuesday — **January 4**

W INTER, with its short days and chilly weather, is not the most popular of seasons. But just think about it for a moment.

Winter weather is a fine excuse for catching up on friends, or clearing a neighbour's snowy path when you are doing your own. Harsher times often seem to bring out the best in us. The Winter of life is often full of deeper understanding, love that is more profound and friendships that have stood the test of time.

Spring and Summer have their own attractions, but as the Scottish writer Samuel Rutherford said, "Grace grows best in the Winter."

AFTER THE RAIN

THE FRIENDSHIP BOOK

Wednesday — **January 5**

HERE are some inspiring words from a French proverb well worth keeping in mind when life is challenging: *Nothing is impossible to a willing heart.*

Thursday — **January 6**

IF there's one chore that the Lady of the House dislikes, it's putting away the Christmas decorations each January.

"Never mind," I said soothingly, as we took down the tree, and repacked the glass baubles. "After all, if every day were a festival, then we'd never appreciate the really special times of year."

The Lady of the House looked thoughtful for a moment then said, "Well, though we may be putting away our decorations, Spring is really just round the corner. Have you seen the snowdrops blooming outside?"

Now that's what I call decorations!

Friday — **January 7**

HERE'S a thought. Our universe is a relatively small one in galactic terms, but it's still huge and one tiny dot of light in that vastness is the star called Antares.

If Antares were a football, the sun would be the size of a full stop. If the sun were football sized, the earth would be a dot. There are billions of people living on the earth and most of it is still empty space.

Now, how big was that problem you were worrying about?

THE FRIENDSHIP BOOK

Saturday — **January 8**

LIFE in "the little house on the prairie" was a constant struggle for survival but it had its compensations. These we can share, even in our modern world.

The following words by Laura Ingalls Wilder are no less true in the town and the city in the twenty-first century than they were on the prairie:

"Life is not intended to be simply a round of work, no matter how interesting or important that work may be. A moment's pause to watch the glory of a sunrise or sunset is soul satisfying, while a bird's song will set the steps to music all day long."

Sunday — **January 9**

I CAME across this unusual version of The Lord's Prayer and would like to share it with you today. Even with such a modern slant, the words remain powerful and filled with life:

O, Breathing Life, your name shines everywhere!
Release a space to plant Your presence here.
Envision Your "I Can" now.
Embody Your desire in every light and form.
Grow through us this moment's bread
and wisdom.
Untie the knots of failure binding us,
As we release the strands we hold of
others' faults.
Help us not to forget our source,
Yet free us from not being in the present.
From you arises every vision, power and song
from gathering to gathering.
Amen.

Monday — *January 10*

WHEN our young friend Jack remarked to his uncle that it seemed as though he'd been waiting forever for his big break as a writer, Uncle Ralph replied with a twinkle in his eye, "Don't wait for your ship to come in, swim out to it."

Wise words, indeed!

Tuesday — *January 11*

FOR me some of the jewels of January are homely things — on a frosty day the comfort of a steaming bowl of soup, fur-lined boots and a warm fleece, a bright fire and a good book or the shelter of a much-loved home when the cold darkness falls.

Other January jewels are things of beauty; the rich green of a holly bush glinting in the rays of a setting sun, a pot of bright flowering bulbs indoors, the enjoyment of a soft, Spring-like day which has somehow managed to wander into January or a snow-covered landscape lit by a full moon.

Then, of course, there is the pleasure of knowing that the shortest day has been and gone, and that the days are slowly but surely lengthening.

Wednesday — *January 12*

WILBUR D. Nesbit said of a smile: "It's worth a million dollars and it doesn't cost a cent." Certainly, a smile costs nothing and have you noticed you often gain something valuable when you give a reciprocal smile?

There are never too many friendly, cheerful faces around, so do keep smiling!

MOUNTAIN HIGH

Thursday — *January 13*

KEEN readers always have books which are never tidied away, simply because they are dipped into so often. Our old friend Mary has many such books and continues to add to her collection, because in the words of Charles Lamb: "I love to lose myself in other men's minds."

Charles Lamb wrote these words in "Detached Thoughts On Books And Reading". He was a poet, essayist and a keen letter writer born in London in 1775 who enjoyed many literary friendships.

Friday — *January 14*

IN the film, "The Four Feathers" Harry Faversham is nearly dead in the midst of a desert when he is found and saved by nomad Abou Fatma.

Faversham wonders why someone would do so much for a stranger. Fatma's reply is simple: "God put you in my way."

What opportunities to help will God put in your way today?

Saturday — *January 15*

ROBERT and Rosa own a new restaurant. After saving for many years, they purchased modest premises, renovated them from top to bottom and later held their grand opening.

The hours are long and the work is hard, but they are thrilled to have their wish finally fulfilled. Rosa has stencilled this quote by Victor Hugo in her fine calligraphy on one of the walls: *There is nothing like a dream to create the future.*

How true!

Sunday — *January 16*

" **I**'M not the right person; I have no idea what to say; can't you find someone else to do it?"

No, these weren't the Lady of the House's excuses, but they could easily have been. Most of us could supply a list just as comprehensive when asked to step out of our comfort zone and help a stranger — or even someone we don't much like!

Luckily Moses put his excuses (for they were his) behind him and stood up to be counted. Next time you feel unable to offer a helping hand or a listening ear — and rest assured that the Bible greats shared your worries and insecurities — try harder to do something about it.

"Then I heard the voice of the Lord saying, 'Whom shall I send? And who will go for us?' And I said, 'Here I am. Send me!'" (Isaiah 6:8)

Monday — *January 17*

*Y*OU plan to thank your loved ones,
  For wisdom that they've taught?
Don't tell them later, tell them now.
  Your friends have kept you going,
With their comfort and support?
  Don't tell them later, tell them now.
For "now" is just the only time
  We're guaranteed to own,
The only time that we might have
  To speak, or write or phone.
So place it high upon your list,
  No matter where or how,
Don't plan for sometime, never —
  Tell them now!
                    Margaret Ingall.

Tuesday — *January 18*

THE Vietnamese have an interesting take on appreciation. "When eating a fruit," an old saying goes, "think of the man who planted the tree."

Imagine if we did that with everything! We might think of the people who grow our food, resurface the roads on which we travel to work, work the power plants that keep our homes warm, pick the tea we drink … the list is endless.

We would soon find we have a lot of things to be thankful for — not such a bad thing, surely, when putting life into perspective.

Wednesday — *January 19*

IN the American Civil War, Colonel "Jeb" Stuart used to end all letters and notes to his commander, Robert E. Lee, with the words, *Yours to count on*.

I can't think of anyone, business acquaintance or friend, I wouldn't want to leave that thought with. And when, in quiet moments throughout the day, we speak to our own Commander we might follow Colonel Stuart's example, re-affirming we are always, *Yours to count on*.

Thursday — *January 20*

ONE day, while browsing in her local library, Joan came across this unusual proverb from Madagascar: *Words are like eggs; when they are hatched they have wings.*

Sound words to keep in mind whenever we're tempted to speak hastily, don't you think?

THE FRIENDSHIP BOOK

Friday — *January 21*

THE power of positive thinking is said to be one of the best ways of achieving a contented life. There are many good things to dwell upon as this simple rhyme suggests:

I made a list of the things I love
And the things that give me pleasure.
It grew and grew and I realise
That my life holds much great treasure.
So now if I'm feeling low
And the world seems so unkind
I glance along my treasure list
And leave my cares behind.

Why not give it a try?

Saturday — *January 22*

MOTHER Teresa was once asked if what she was doing for the poor wasn't just a drop in the ocean. "Yes," she agreed, "but it takes many drops to make the ocean."

Sunday — *January 23*

JANUARY may often begin with a sparkle, but for many people its grey skies and long nights can make it feel that Winter darkness will never end. As ever, the Bible has words to encourage us:

"God is light, and in Him is no darkness at all."
(John1 1:15)

"The rising sun will come to us from heaven to shine on those who live in darkness."
(Luke1:78-79)

Let these words illuminate your life.

Monday — *January 24*

FRIENDSHIP as a habit? I'd never thought of it that way before. Eustace Budgell, who was a seventeenth-century man of letters, is recorded as saying, "Friendship is a strong and habitual inclination in two people to promote the good and happiness of one another."

That's one good habit we can all cultivate — now!

Tuesday — *January 25*

LETTIE Cowman supported her husband in missionary work in the Far East until his failing health forced them to return home. After nursing him for six years, at the age of fifty-three Lettie found herself a widow.

Many people would have been content to live a quiet life thinking that their best days were behind them. But Lettie drew on her experiences to write the inspirational classic, "Streams In The Desert" and seven other books besides.

"Some lives, like evening primroses, blossom most beautifully in the evening of life," she reminds us.

Wednesday — *January 26*

FRENCH author and aviator Antoine De Saint-Exupery said, "A rock pile ceases to be a rock pile the moment a single man contemplates it, bearing within him the image of a cathedral."

A clever and memorable insight that can be applied to many of life's challenges, don't you agree?

Thursday — *January 27*

ARCHBISHOP Desmond Tutu has told a light-hearted story about the time he met Nelson Mandela soon after his release from prison. It was known he didn't like Nelson Mandela's choice of shirts, because he thought they looked rather like pyjamas.

The Archbishop was greatly amused to learn that Mandela had retorted, "But this, coming from a man who wears a dress in public!"

As Mark Twain once said, "Humour is the great thing, the saving thing. The minute it crops up, all our irritations and resentments slip away and a sunny spirit takes their place."

Friday — *January 28*

HERE are some wise words from a Japanese proverb to consider today: *Fall seven times, stand up eight.*

Saturday — *January 29*

DO you ever get bored doing the same old thing day after day? You cut the grass — and it grows again. You wash dishes — and they are used again in no time. You go to work — and have to go back again the next day.

It can get you down. Or you could look at it like St Therese of Lisieux. She said, "Every small task of everyday life is part of the total harmony of the universe."

So you're not really weeding the garden or cleaning the floor for the umpteenth time this week. You're keeping the universe in harmony!

Sunday — *January 30*

O N some older sets of binoculars there is a metal button between the two eye-pieces. It's basically the head of a threaded bolt, and turning it adjusts the focus of the binoculars. On some the words *Turn To Clear Vision* are printed.

Focus can be a problem in the modern world. We have so many things clamouring for our attention it can be easy to lose sight of what is important. If we turn to God, though, our vision will be cleared. We will see through all the distractions and focus on what really matters.

"Look to the Lord and his strength; seek his face always." (Chronicles1 16:11)

Monday — *January 31*

H OLD fast to dreams
For dreamers see tomorrow,
Keep safe your wishes,
Wishes can come true.
Let faith be strong
To hold you in the sadness,
Reach out for love
And love will see you through.

Be light of heart
The world is full of wonder,
Go bravely on
Whatever comes your way.
Have hope and courage,
Life has much to offer,
Reach out for love
And love will light the day.
Iris Hesselden.

February

HAVE you heard of the charity called Music In Hospitals? Since it was founded in 1948 it has arranged numerous concerts in hospitals, care homes, hospices and day centres in many parts of the United Kingdom.

Musicians and singers who have taken part say they are richly rewarded by the response of their listeners.

"To see their faces light up gives us so much joy," said one singer. "Of course they can hear music on the radio or television but a live performance gives them so much more."

Nursing staff agree and say the concerts give their patients a real lift. In one Glasgow hospital a woman spoke for the first time in forty years.

Music can indeed heal.

THE little tree, while yet so small,
Withstands the Winter's blast,
For though it bends beneath the storm
Its roots hold firm and fast.
So like that tree, let's try our best
To root in all that's strong,
For love and truth can hold us safe
Throughout our whole life long.
                    Margaret Ingall.

22

Thursday — *February 3*

HERE'S something to think about today. Without olives being squeezed there would be no olive oil. Without grapes being pressed there would be no wine. Without the dough being kneaded bread wouldn't rise.

So if you are feeling a little under pressure, don't worry – it's just God bringing out the best in you!

Friday — *February 4*

WHAT could be more useless than a pocket with the bottom worn out? It might still be able to keep your hand warm but as for fulfilling its original purpose, well . . .

But, wait, there is another – excellent – use for it. According to a wise old proverb there is no other place half as well suited for keeping your troubles in than the pocket with holes in it!

Saturday — *February 5*

NOT so many people have an open fire in their living-room nowadays. Our friend Bill still does, though, and as we sat toasting our toes one day at the warm glow of burning logs, he told me why.

"They say that man first learned to make fire all of 790,000 years ago. He has been using it ever since. When I hold my hands out to my fire I feel at one with all these generations of men, women and children over the years. The thought gives me a warm feeling inside as well as out."

Bill lives alone but, thanks to his imagination, when he is sitting by his fireside he always has company.

Sunday — *February 6*

THERE'S an African saying that translates as, "Oh, Lord, you are the needle and I am the thread."

This puzzled me for a while, but then I realised that the needle does not hold up the hems of my trousers, the needle does not keep the buttons attached to my shirt. The thread does all the work — work it could not possibly have done if it hadn't been following the needle.

"Whoever serves me must follow me; and where I am my servant also will be. My father will honour the one who serves me." (John 12:26)

Monday — *February 7*

WHEN Monica was taken into hospital with a broken ankle, she wasn't expecting an easy convalescence when she arrived home. The house next door had just been let to a group of lively young folk and she feared that noise might disturb her. But as soon as they learned of her predicament, she found her assumptions had been wrong.

"Straight away they came round offering to do my shopping, run errands, and keep the garden tidy. In fact, I'm not sure what was worse," she joked wryly, "being ill or having to rethink all my prejudices!"

As Monica discovered, learning about others can often teach us a great deal about ourselves, and it isn't always easy. Indeed, her words put me in mind of those written by poet Kahlil Gibran: "Your pain is the breaking of the shell that encloses your understanding."

And once we are released from that shell, just see how we can grow!

TREASURE IN THE WOODS

Tuesday — *February 8*

I HAVE been reading about a time capsule for the digital age. Instead of burying pictures, letters and similar keepsakes in a box and hoping they will be discovered in the future, now you can write yourself an e-mail and it will be delivered back to you in five, ten or twenty years time.

What would you write? And what would you expect to have changed in all that time? Well, I'm going to make a guess. I'd say the worries that loom so large right now would be long forgotten by then. But the things you value, the things you love, will still make your heart sing, no matter when that digital time capsule comes back.

Wednesday — *February 9*

IN the 1950 issue of "Scouting Magazine" Forest Witcraft wrote, "A hundred years from now it will not matter what my bank account was, the sort of house I lived in, or the kind of car I drove. But the world may be different, because I was important in the life of a young person."

Children are the future of the world and they will learn by watching us. So let's follow this example and take the time — it may only need a smile or an encouraging word — to show them the value of kindness and love.

Thursday — *February 10*

TIME is like a river. You can't touch the same water twice because the flow that has passed will never pass again. So enjoy every moment of your life.

Friday — *February 11*

I REMEMBER the Lady of the House once telling me that she felt friendship was a bit like being on a see-saw: "Sometimes you're up, sometimes you're down, but at least you know you're never on your own!"

William A. Ward puts it more elegantly: "A true friend knows your weaknesses but shows you your strengths; feels your fears but fortifies your faith; sees your anxieties but frees your spirit; recognises your disabilities but emphasises your possibilities."

That's a partnership that really will cushion the bumps!

Saturday — *February 12*

THE new year lies behind us, Lord,
 The time is moving on,
With many resolutions now
 Forgotten, lost and gone.
But through the months before us, Lord,
 Please help us to be strong,
Protect us in the storms of life
 When we are blown along.

And through the promise of the Spring,
 The warmth of Summer days,
Remind us we are truly blessed
 In, oh, so many ways.
The year has much to offer, Lord,
 And lessons we must learn,
Now help us plant new seeds of hope
 As all the seasons turn.

Iris Hesselden.

LOOK OF LOVE

THE FRIENDSHIP BOOK

Sunday — *February 13*

THERE is a story written by an unknown author of a sick man who asked his doctor what lies on the other side. His doctor said he didn't know.

The man replied, "You are a Christian, yet you do not know what is on the other side?"

The doctor stood by the door of the sitting-room; from the hall came the sounds of scratching and whining. When he opened the door a dog leaped into the room, barking joyfully and wagging its tail.

Turning to his patient, he said, "My dog didn't know what to expect in this room, only that his master was here and when the door opened, he sprang in without fear. I know little of what is on the other side, but I do know one thing. I know my Master is there and that is enough."

"In my Father's house are many mansions: if it were not so, I would have told you. I go to prepare a place for you."   (John 14:2)

Monday — *February 14*

THERE is an old custom in Wales of giving your sweetheart a love spoon. From as early as the seventeenth century young men were carving a spoon to give to their intended. If their beloved accepted it, they became engaged and she would always treasure the spoon.

The handles were often carved with intricate symbols of love and affection, and many of them are considered real works of art nowadays.

In recent years Welsh woodcarvers have been reviving this custom and finding ready sales, so old-fashioned romance is surely still alive and well!

29

Tuesday — **February 15**

THE Lady of the House is very attentive when it comes to dusting and cleaning. Any spiders' webs in my bookroom window are all swept away, and usually I admit to her that I didn't even notice they were there to begin with.

But what I find amazing is just how quickly the spiders return to rebuild their webs. They never give up — they just begin again. How much they can teach us all about faith and perseverance.

Wednesday — **February 16**

WINNING WORDS

SAY to someone something kind
Speak praise sincerely meant,
Express appreciation
And give encouragement.
For we inspire and influence,
Just through the words we say,
Within us lies the power to bless
And change somebody's day.
Kathleen Gillum.

Thursday — **February 17**

I WAS astounded to discover that the statue of a winged man with a bow in the centre of Piccadilly Circus isn't really called Eros. Apparently Eros is just a popular misnaming of this work of art, which is actually called The Angel Of Christian Charity.

But then, I shouldn't be surprised. After all, charity at its best usually goes in disguise, doing its purest work without the recipients ever knowing it was there.

Friday — *February 18*

DO not look at the faults of what others have done or not done; observe what you yourself have done or not done.

Buddha.

Saturday — *February 19*

THE Lady of the House and I enjoy reading Great-Aunt Louisa's scrapbooks and diaries, and we like to share their contents with you. On one occasion Louisa wrote:

February 19th. — "It has been a long, cold Winter with heavy snowfalls, and several times frost patterns on the inside of my bedroom window hastened me to light the fire. But today I was surprised by a gentle blue sky, and pale sunshine.

"Never more so than on such a day, do we think of the sun in the words of William Henley as 'an influence luminous, serene. A shining peace . . .' and lift our faces to it. There are signs of Spring all around — silvery buds on my magnolia tree promising pink-flushed flowers, a small drift of snowdrops under the plum tree, and there are early hazel catkins down by the stream.

"All these things remind us that the landscape in Winter is not one of decline, but rather one of rest for the new season of Spring. But now the light has gone, I will in the manner of the writer William Cowper 'stir the fire, and close the shutters fast, let fall the curtains, wheel the sofa round', make tea, and 'welcome peaceful evening in'."

A small watercolour of a snowdrop, a catkin and a blue tit illustrates this entry, and beside it are these words: "Single snowdrops have a delicate, sweet scent of honey."

Sunday — *February 20*

JESUS' parable of the Prodigal Son might be called the Little Bible for the whole message of Christianity is in that story. Even though the young and foolish son leaves home not caring one jot for his father or the rest of his family, his father welcomes him with loving arms when at last he returns home.

What a wonderful picture this is of a loving God who always forgives us and never stops loving us: "But while he was still a long way off, his father saw him and was filled with compassion for him; he ran to his son, threw his arms around him and kissed him."   (Luke 15:20)

Monday — *February 21*

OUR Canadian friend Tom couldn't understand why each Winter the bird feeders in his backyard were deserted. He filled them with all sorts of seeds and treats, but very few birds came.

Finally, his neighbour advised him to surround his feeders with branches and greenery to give the birds a sense of security. He told Tom that because most trees in Winter have lost their cover, feeders are exposed, leaving birds vulnerable to predators.

So Tom cut some fresh cedar boughs and arranged them around his feeders. The birds came almost immediately — cardinals, chickadees, finches, woodpeckers, nuthatches, even a family of blue jays — all swooped down to feast together in a noisy celebration.

Now, isn't that a little like life? There's nothing quite as wonderful as the company of friends in a warm, safe place!

CLEAR AS CRYSTAL

Tuesday — *February 22*

" **I** OFTEN wish," our old friend Mary said, "that I had more hours in the day just for myself, space to be quiet and reflect on life."

There are many occasions when we dream of taking tranquil time out of our busy lives. However, what we shouldn't forget is that we don't have to go away or be in a special place to achieve this.

Going for a walk, sitting on a bench in a park for a while, or even just relaxing at home listening to favourite music can all provide a quiet corner. A magazine article even said that one of our favourite thinking places is in a car or bus — not so surprising when you consider how many hours can be spent in a vehicle.

So next time you long to be alone with your thoughts for a little while during a busy day, remember that it doesn't have to be an impossible dream. Sanctuary can simply be wherever we are willing to find it.

Wednesday — *February 23*

" **T** HE creation of a thousand forests is in one acorn," wrote Ralph Waldo Emerson. Think about it for a moment . . .

One acorn grows one tree. That tree grows hundreds of acorns, each capable of growing a new tree and each new tree, in turn, brings a new batch of acorns. Left undisturbed, those trees could eventually cover the world!

Now, tell me, which do you think is the more powerful, which has the greater potential when it comes to changing the world — an acorn? Or an act of love.

THE FRIENDSHIP BOOK

Thursday — **February 24**

THE Bible story happened such a long time ago that it can seem very remote. However, when you think about it, the people of Biblical times had the same faults and weaknesses as ourselves — jealousy, greed and selfishness were common, but so were kindness, courage and generosity.

Read the Bible with this in mind and you realise that the God of Abraham, Isaac and Jacob is today the God of Tom, Dick and Harry. Yes, and of Nan, Jean and Katy, too.

Friday — **February 25**

*COME away with me
And we'll let starlight run
through our fingers
Like gossamer sand;
We'll shine the northern lights into night's
    dim corners
And unravel mysteries;
We'll dress up in moonbeams
And laugh and dance.
Although the hour is late,
This is not a time for sleep;
This is a time to discover,
To dare,
To ask why not.
Come away, dear friend,
While we can still step over the lintel
Into magic,
Believing that dreams are within reach,
Surprises are waiting to be unwrapped
And a falling star makes your wish come true.*
                                Rachel Wallace–Oberle.

Saturday — *February 26*

HAVE you niggling doubts about something new you are about to embark on? It could, you might be thinking, suffer a setback or two, or even be unsuccessful.

Well, don't give up because all life is a mixture of successes and failures, whatever we are doing. Keep in mind these wise words from the pen of George William Curtis:

"It is not the ship so much as skilful sailing that ensures the prosperous voyage". With a bit of perseverance, your undertaking will most likely be a successful one.

Sunday — *February 27*

GALATIANS 6:2

"BEAR ye one another's burdens",
Thus the Bible so commends,
Bidding us to help our neighbours,
Care for strangers as our friends.
For we all are brothers, sisters,
Children of our Lord above.
Let us learn by His example:
Fill the world with gifts of love.

M. J. Brison.

Monday — *February 28*

W. H. AUDEN wrote: "We are here to serve others. What the others are here for, I don't know."

It's a wry comment on how life can appear when you are doing your best — but seem to be the only one! Never mind, just remember that the most important sentence in that quote is the first one.

March

A YOUNG man in a poem by Alfred Lord Tennyson says: "What shall I be at fifty, should nature keep me alive, if I find the world so bitter when I am but twenty-five."

I like the cheerful parody of this which asks: "What shall I be at ninety, if nature keeps me alive, when I find the world so sweet and jolly, when I'm only eighty-five!"

It is, as they say, all in the mind.

A WEEK of frost, of fog and cold
  But then the sun came out,
And like a ray of new-born hope
  It brushed away the doubt.

A week of gales and heavy rain
  But then the wind grew calm,
And like the peace of silent hills
  It spread a healing balm.

A week of floods and melting snow
  But then the earth revealed,
The wonder of awaking Spring
  In every tree and field!

Iris Hesselden.

Thursday — **March 3**

" **I**F a child is to keep their inborn sense of wonder they need the companionship of at least one adult who can share it, rediscovering with them the joy, excitement and mystery of the world we live in."

She didn't mean to but when Rachel Carson wrote this I think she may just have written the perfect job description for the post of Grandparent!

Friday — **March 4**

WHICH do you think is the best character trait to encourage in the younger generation? Biographer Nancy Mitford was in no doubt that it should be patience.

"I think young people have the feeling life is slipping past them and they must do something – they don't quite know what, whereas they've only got to wait – it all comes. What's so nice and so unexpected about life is the way it improves as it goes along."

Words well worth thinking about, surely.

Saturday — **March 5**

EACH Spring as she ventures out to re-acquaint herself with the delights of her garden our old friend Mary recalls these words of H. Fred Ale. Perhaps they stay in mind because they are as relevant to relationships with people as they are to relationships with gardens.

"My green thumb," he wrote, "only came as a result of the mistakes I made while learning to see

Sunday — *March 6*

THERE'S no doubt about it — modern life can be a tiring, non-stop whirl of activity and our bodies can become weary, our minds somewhat jaded. Perhaps when we feel in need of a little spiritual refreshment, we could keep these words from Isaiah 30:31 in mind:

"Those who hope in the Lord will renew their strength. They will soar on wings like eagles; they will run and not grow weary, they will walk and not be faint."

So today, may you fly on the wings of faith, knowing that you can never fall beyond His reach.

Monday — *March 7*

"OH dear," the Lady of the House said as she put down the phone. "Joyce can't meet me. Still, at least her call saved me a fruitless wait in the rain. Thank goodness for Alexander Graham Bell."

Born in Scotland in 1847, Bell's early interest in the science of speech was not surprising, for his mother was deaf and his father the inventor of a code called Visible Speech showing the way that throat, lips and tongue work to produce sound.

Bell shared his father's gifts, for he himself overcame illness and lack of education to invent not just the telephone but other things, including a hydrofoil and a device for locating icebergs.

But it will always be the telephone for which he is best remembered. Despite occasional grumbles at its summons, there's no doubt that the ability to communicate instantly over any distance has not just saved lives and united friends and family; it

Tuesday — **March 8**

HOWARD, a neighbour, recently retired from his job so I was interested to see how he was enjoying his new leisure time.

"Well," he told me, "when I was young, my grandfather was always quoting that old proverb: *One of these days is none of these days.* It did remind me to work hard and never to put off what needed to be done.

"However, on the day I retired my wife found me this quotation from the writer Douglas Pagels: 'Sometimes it's important to work for that pot of gold. But other times it's essential to take time off to make sure that your most important decision of the day simply consists of choosing which colour to slide down on the rainbow'."

Howard grinned. "So today I'm just polishing up my sliding skills!"

Wednesday — **March 9**

HERE are some brave words from Martin Luther King, who died from an assassin's bullet:

"Cowardice asks the question — is it safe? Expediency asks the question — is it popular? But conscience asks the question — is it right? And there comes a time when one must take a position that is neither safe, nor politic, nor popular, but one must take it because it is right."

Thursday — **March 10**

I READ these philosophical words from the Indian writer N. Sri Ram in a book of thought-provoking quotations: "There is no wisdom without love."

Friday — *March 11*

I'M sure we would all like to be thought of as a good listener but so often we mean well, we intend to keep quiet and to give our companion our full attention — but then there is a small pause, and we rush in, assuming we know just how the other person feels.

That's why I particularly appreciate the words of radio producer Neenah Ellis, who devoted a year to travelling around, listening to and recording centenarians speaking of all the events they had lived through. She said:

"There is a universe in the sound of every voice, and if you're a patient listener you can often sense the heartbeat in the long silences between the words."

Now that's the sort of listener we would all like to talk to.

Saturday — *March 12*

" IT'S a rare and lucky person who never gets fed up with life," our friend Ted observed. "So when my spirits need a lift, I visit the local arboretum. You know, I could spend hours just wandering among the trees, and I always feel so much better for it."

Writer Marcel Proust would have agreed: "We have nothing to fear and a great deal to learn from trees, that vigorous and pacific tribe which without stint produces strengthening essences for us, soothing balms, and in whose gracious company we spend so many cool, silent and intimate hours."

There's a man who could certainly see the wood for the trees!

Sunday — *March 13*

EVERYTHING we do has consequences so why should prayer be any different? The sixteenth-century preacher Robert Sibbes saw it this way:

"When we shoot an arrow, we look for the fall of it; when we send a ship out to sea, we look for the return of it; when we sow seed, we look for a harvest: and so when we sow our prayers into God's bosom, shall we not look for an answer?"

"For everyone who asks, receives; he who seeks, finds; and to him who knocks, the door will be opened."   (Matthew 7:8)

Monday — *March 14*

FROM the days when there was a different Western showing at the cinema every week come these words of advice.

Usually the older, more worldly-wise cowboy would tell his younger companion, "When you get to where you're going, the first thing you do is take care of the horse."

It's a reminder that none of us travel through this world on our own, and even if we don't have a horse to rub down we can always give thanks to those who helped us on our way.

Tuesday — *March 15*

SOMETIMES we put up with behaviour from loved ones we would never accept from more casual acquaintances. Why do we do that? Well, the old saying is that "Love is blind", but I believe the eyes of love see more clearly than others and make allowances.

Wednesday — **March 16**

NOWADAYS we are all aware that many species of life are endangered. One who early saw the warning signs and how precious all growing things are was the biologist Bruce Frederick Cummings, who was born in 1889.

An entry in his diary reads: "Give me the man who will surrender the whole world for a moss or a caterpillar."

Fortunately, there are many people today who share his passion and are dedicated to saving Nature's precious bounty.

Thursday — **March 17**

WHILE browsing in our bookroom I came across this Jewish prayer for well-being and I hope you'll enjoy sharing its gentle words today:

May the source of strength who blessed the ones before us help us find the courage to make our lives a blessing.

And let us say, Amen.

Friday — **March 18**

SOCRATES has become known the whole world over as a philosopher and a wise man, but according to French Renaissance writer Michel de Montaigne his real claim to fame should perhaps have been something altogether different.

"There is nothing more notable in Socrates," he wrote, "than that he found time when he was an old man to learn music and dancing – and thought it time well spent."

So the next time someone tells us to act our age, let's act Socrates' age instead!

THE GOLDEN PATH

Saturday — *March 19*

IRIS loved cats – and didn't her grandchildren just know it! For years, at every birthday and Christmas, she received gifts of cats in every possible combination: tea towels, tea cosies, calendars, cards, jewellery and, of course, ornaments. But as the collection grew and grew, the time eventually came to do a little tidying out.

Each present was a reminder of something much more precious than the pets Iris adores – her nine grandchildren and their love for her.

Much as she craved more space and less dusting, she couldn't bring herself to get rid of all those carefully chosen presents, so after much thought she had a brainwave. The cats would be carefully rotated round the house, and one by one, each would enjoy a special time in the limelight, before being put away for a while.

And her grandchildren? Well, they're in the spotlight all the time, because as Iris knows, it's people, not things, that matter most.

Sunday — *March 20*

A NEW social club opened not long ago in our friend Norma's village and one of its recommendations is that members should try to avoid all idle gossip and chit chat about people and, of course, about fellow members!

Now, isn't that a grand idea? Surely one to be commended everywhere – at home, at work and while we are at leisure. As we are reminded in Proverbs 20:19:

"Gossip betrays confidence; avoid men who talk too much."

Monday — *March 21*

COUNTRY singer Dolly Parton may sing the occasional sad song but in real life she is relentlessly upbeat and optimistic. You may wonder why. Well, you could say it's down to forward planning.

"I wake up every day expecting it to be good," she said, "and if it's not I set about trying to get it fixed. I try to live every day like it might be my last. I don't want to have to wake up, face God and say, 'Well, duh, I should have tried'."

Now, that's the way to plan a life!

Tuesday — *March 22*

I PAUSE on the footbridge and gaze at
  the stream
So often I stop here, to stand and to dream,
I watch as the water goes dimple-dance by
Reflecting the sun and the blue of the sky.
A dragonfly skims on a rainbow of light,
A ribbon of minnows slides swiftly from sight.
A blackbird is singing, bright notes fill the air
The water runs chuckling, bereft of all care —
It's just an oasis of coolness and calm
A welcome small moment of Nature's soft balm.

Margaret Ingall.

Wednesday — *March 23*

THERE have been many words in this book about friendship over the years, and I particularly like this definition of a friend:

"A friend is someone who goes around saying nice things about you behind your back."

ARE YOU LISTENING?

Thursday — **March 24**

WE'D all like to be perfect, wouldn't we? Well, here's a story of a Chinese peasant who collected water every day with the same two jugs.

One jug was perfect but the other had a crack and leaked all the way back from the river. The perfect jug did the right thing and carried water properly, but a line of flowers came to grow in the dust where the cracked jug had left a trickle of water every day.

Perfection would be fine, but it's the cracks, the flaws, the different personality traits that make the world a more colourful place!

Friday — **March 25**

JOHN F. Kennedy spoke these thought-provoking words in 1959: "We should not let our fears hold us back from pursuing our hopes."

Wise words well worth keeping in mind.

Saturday — **March 26**

JOE is the man who keeps our local streets clean and what a good job he makes! There is never as much as a piece of paper to be seen after he has been working.

The other day I spotted him as he was shovelling a pile of rubbish someone had left at the entrance to our park.

"That's terrible, Joe," I said. "Some people are so thoughtless."

He looked up from his work and grinned. "Well, the way I look at it is this — if they were as tidy as you and me, I'd be out of a job!"

Sunday — March 27

THE great writer H. G. Wells was a keen student of human nature and made this observation:

"Until a man has found God, and been found by God," he wrote, "he begins at no beginning, he works to no end. He may have his friendships, partial loyalties and scraps of honour, but all these things fall into place — and life falls into place — only with God."

"But I said, 'I have laboured to no purpose; I have spent my strength in vain and for nothing. Yet what is due me is in the Lord's hand, and my reward is with my God'." (Isaiah 49:4)

Monday — March 28

NIGHT has washed the old day clean
  And all is fresh and new,
As dawn arrives on slippered feet
  And scatters pearls of dew.
The clouds are bathed in rosy tints
  Which change before the eye,
As morning light in golden beams
  Streams out across the sky.

The world wakes up and starts to stir
  The skylark's on the wing,
From feathered throats come fluted notes —
  A choir begins to sing.
And all of Nature springs to life
  With rising of the sun,
And starts to sing her song of joy
  A new day has begun.
                    Kathleen Gillum.

Tuesday — **March 29**

THERE are very few occupations or interests that could accommodate if everyone wanted to get involved in them. But there is one, described eloquently by Charles Dickens, that we might wish the whole world would pursue.

"I feel an earnest and humble desire," the great novelist wrote, "and shall till I die, to increase the stock of harmless cheerfulness."

Wednesday — **March 30**

AT our young friends' wedding, this unusual grace was said before the bride and groom and their guests sat down to eat:

As Jesus blessed the loaves and fishes,
Bless the food upon our dishes,
And like the sugar in our tea,
May we be all stirred up by Thee.

Words from the heart that the assembled guests will remember for a long time.

Thursday — **March 31**

PRINCE Albert met with some suspicion from the British public when he married Queen Victoria.

However, in the years that followed they grew to respect and admire him as a tower of strength for their monarch, always by her side giving her the companionship and quiet support she needed as she handled great affairs of state.

As for Albert, his love for Victoria deepened over the years and when he died in 1861 he said on his deathbed, "I have had wealth, rank and power, but if these were all I had, how wretched I should be."

April

Friday — **April 1**

IT'S Spring and daffodils and crocuses are blooming, birds are making nests, trees are in bud and the grass is turning a deeper shade of green.

Spring reminds me of these beautiful words from the Talmud: *Every blade of grass has its angel that bends over it and whispers, "Grow, grow!"*

When you step outside today, look around for a few moments and let the message of Nature's simple things speak to you.

Saturday — **April 2**

ONE day in 1889 a young author sat down to write a book. "I did not intend to write a funny one," he said later. "I did not know I was a humorist."

It was to be called "The Story Of The Thames" but it became one of the most amusing and best-loved books in the English language, "Three Men In A Boat".

Jerome K. Jerome never understood why it was so popular and thought some of his other books were far better. Boating on the Thames, he said, was his favourite hobby and "I just put down the things that happened on our trip."

After all these years this simple tale of three friends and a dog is still making readers laugh.

Sunday — *April 3*

PAUL'S computer had a substantial "Temporary Files" folder. These pages were once current and important but went out of date, serving only to slow everything down. Once the list was deleted, however, his computer seemed to take on a new lease of life.

How many pointless old grudges and thoughtless acts do each of us carry around in our memories, serving no purpose but to slow our spirits down? Wouldn't it be better if we could just press "Delete"?

"Bear with each other and forgive whatever grievances you may have against one another. Forgive as the Lord forgave you." (Colossians 3:13)

Monday — *April 4*

WE cannot choose our challenges,
For most times they choose us.
We cannot pick the easy ones
That cause no fret or fuss.
And sometimes we meet troubles
That seem to overwhelm,
We feel adrift in stormy seas,
No hand upon the helm,
Yet somewhere in the darkness
A steady light shines clear,
To warn us of the danger,
To show which way to steer.
So though we may feel helpless,
And small and weak inside,
Remember, just by asking,
We'll always find a Guide.

Margaret Ingall.

Tuesday — **April 5**

YOU might think that Charles Dickens was speaking of the impossible when he wrote: "Have a heart that never hardens, a temper that never tires, and a touch that never hurts."

After all, what man or woman could hope to achieve that impossible standard? But before we dismiss his advice as unrealistic, perhaps we should stop a moment and ask, which of us would not benefit from trying?

Wednesday — **April 6**

"WELL, that's when I gave him (or her) a piece of my mind!" How many times have you heard that said? And you can guarantee that while it may have made the speaker feel better, it probably left the situation worse!

That's why I would like to pass on these anonymous words of wisdom: "We'd all be happier if we gave others a piece of our heart instead of a piece of our mind."

Thursday — **April 7**

OUR friend Maureen always seems to be cheerful and smiling and, when asked about her philosophy for dealing with the everyday problems we all encounter, she said:

"Well, when things get tough, I always remember that my faith will not get me around trouble but it will get me through it — and I find that it always does."

With such conviction, is it little wonder that she

Friday — *April 8*

IN the course of the nineteenth century, the magnificent osprey — or fish hawk — was hunted to extinction in Scotland. Then, during the 1960s, two birds returned, built a nest and raised fledglings.

This time people did all they could to encourage the osprey's recovery. Today, there are many pairs of these birds all across Scotland and they are now breeding in northern England once more. Nature is strong indeed, with the power to recover over and over again.

Saturday — *April 9*

I CAME across these words by Charlotte Brontë, and they make a good thought for today:

"If we would build on a sure foundation in friendship we must love our friends for their sakes rather than our own."

Sunday — *April 10*

THERE'S a little-known planning regulation in Washington D.C., that decrees no building is allowed to be raised to a height higher than the Washington Monument. Ask a planner why and they might say it's just one of those things.

But on the stainless steel peak of the monument, and visible only from above, are the words, *Laus Deo*, "Praise be to God."

I think the original town planners who laid down those laws were right. After all, what should be higher than that?

"I will proclaim the name of the Lord. Oh, praise the greatness of our God!"   (Deuteronomy 32:3)

NOW THE DAY IS OVER

Monday — *April 11*

NO doubt we have all felt at times that we'd like to be enjoying some leisure time far away from daily routine and not least, during weeks when cold and wet weather seem never ending.

Milton Berle, the television and film comedian, had an idea that I'd like to share. "Laughter," he said, "is an instant vacation." It's true, isn't it?

When someone makes you laugh, it takes you to a wonderful place, no matter where you might be at that moment. And, if that someone is a friend, then you can go on holiday together, even if only for a little while.

Tuesday — *April 12*

I WISH you the beauty of Nature
The joy of the sun on the sea,
The wonder and magic of Springtime
And all that tomorrow can be.
I wish you fresh hope every morning
And friends who will share the new day,
A rainbow to shine through the storm clouds
And flowers to dance on your way.

I wish you deep peace and contentment
Warm memories lifting your heart,
The courage of all your convictions
Whenever you make a new start.
I wish you these gifts and these blessings
And strength to go on, walking tall,
And love in abundance around you
For love is the greatest of all!

Iris Hesselden.

Wednesday — *April 13*

OUR old friend Mary usually celebrates her birthday in style, but although the Lady of the House and I were invited, as usual, to her tea-party, I noticed that Mary didn't seem quite as enthusiastic as usual about the event.

"I'm afraid that the next one will be a 'big' birthday," she said, smiling, "and somehow, it does seem to emphasise the passing of the years."

The Lady of the House laughed. "Then I have just the right quotation for you from good old Mr Anon: *A birthday is just the first day of another three hundred and sixty four-day journey round the sun.*"

"Hmm," mused Mary. "The start of a journey. Now that sounds much more exciting. There's nothing I like better than a new beginning."

I can't help thinking that our friend's birthday celebrations will be as joyful as ever next year!

Thursday — *April 14*

I WAS rather taken aback when our friend Andrew told me his Golden Rule. Each day he does his very best to drink, steal, swear and lie, he said with a straight face.

I looked puzzled, but then he explained, "I drink from the everlasting cup of faith each day. I try my best to steal five minutes each day to do something for someone in need. I swear to myself that I will be a better person tomorrow than I was today. And as I 'lie' down each night I thank God for the day that's just been."

Oh, now, that's altogether different, then!

Friday — **April 15**

I'VE heard many definitions of optimists and pessimists, usually involving glasses of water that are either half full or half empty, but that idea was turned on its head by a friend recently.

"An optimist," he said, "takes the cold water the pessimist poured on his idea, heats it with his enthusiasm and uses the steam to drive that idea ahead."

Wise words worth remembering!

Saturday — **April 16**

IF you had walked with me today
On rain-washed roads hemmed with buttercups,
Fresh and dripping,
You would have witnessed Grace.

If you had crossed the field with me today
And bent to drink
From a stream choked with brilliance in the sun,
You would have witnessed Grace.

If you had stood with me tonight
Upon the darkened lawn,
And reached for starry lamps hung in
*   the heavens,*
You would have witnessed Grace.

Grace composes glory on the earth,
Paints grandeur in the sky,
Pours majesty into the dancing azure deeps;
His tender thoughts —
Shouting to be heard.

                                    Rachel Wallace–Oberle.

*Sunday — **April 17***

NEAR Land's End in Cornwall there's a building with a plaque outside which says: *This is the last house in England . . . and the first!*

Of course it all depends which way you turn. Go in the direction of the cliffs and it's the last, walk towards the mainland and it's the first.

In the same way, when you reach "the last straw" or blow your "last chance" you can turn towards despair and give up, or you can turn towards help and begin a whole new adventure.

"Turn to me and be saved, all you ends of the earth: for I am God and there is no other."

(Isaiah 45:22)

*Monday — **April 18***

PUSH ups, pull ups, sit ups . . . We all know that regular exercise is important for our wellbeing but our friend Helen much prefers to take the advice of the early twentieth-century physician and writer John Andrew Holmes:

"There is no exercise better for the heart than reaching down and lifting people up."

*Tuesday — **April 19***

WE live in an aspirational, often competitive world. Lots of people want to have lifestyles like famous sports or film stars. But there is an old Yiddish proverb that puts all that into perspective:

"If I try to be like him, who will be like me?"

We all have faults but despite that each of us is unique. When it comes to being you, there is no one in the whole world who could do the job half as well as you!

Wednesday — **April 20**

NANDI is a young woman from the busy Indian city of Delhi. In a letter to a friend she described the hectic pace of modern life, with these thoughtful words at the end.

"Often in this life," she wrote, "we are running so fast we don't have time to notice those running along beside us. We only notice when we fall — and they stop to pick us up."

Thursday — **April 21**

WITH a mature, worldly-wise and serious head on I could declare that daydreaming is a waste of time. Working hard is surely the only way to get ahead.

But my frivolous side then asks, why do so many of us indulge in wishful thinking so often? And where would we be without dreams?

Author and philosopher Henry David Thoreau might have found a way to satisfy both sides of the coin when he wrote:

"If you have built castles in the air your work need not be lost; that is where they should be. Now put foundations underneath them."

Friday — **April 22**

PROBABLY not many people would immediately associate the bloodstone, or heliotrope, with the Crucifixion, yet there is an old tradition which says that the red spots of this precious stone were caused by the Blood of Christ falling on a piece of crystal lying at the foot of the Cross.

Saturday — *April 23*

" JUST stop and take a look at that view!" Ella said to her friend Nell one day.

They had been walking along the old railway track, a path they had followed many times but now, halted by Ella's words, Nell gazed across to see the distant hills lit by the late afternoon sunshine — it was a sight to make the heart sing, and yet she admitted that she hadn't even really noticed it.

Leo Buscaglia was a wise man, and tried never to take such everyday things for granted as these words show: "The fact that I can plant a seed and it becomes a flower, share a bit of knowledge and it becomes another's, smile at someone and receive a smile in return, are to me continual spiritual exercises."

And a joy as well!

Sunday — *April 24*

MANY of the great painters turned their brushes to a depiction of the crucifixion. Each brought quite a different interpretation to their picture, but Rembrandt went one step further.

Behind the two guards at the foot of the cross can be seen the face of a man rumoured to be Rembrandt himself. It was the painter's way of saying Jesus didn't just die for everyone, he died for Rembrandt personally and each of us individually.

"May I never boast except in the cross of our Lord Jesus Christ, through which the world has been crucified to me, and I to the world."

Monday — *April 25*

THE beautiful hummingbird is famed for being able to hover in mid-air. It can even fly backwards, something no other bird can do. But it wouldn't exist but for its elongated beak which enables it to feed from deep within a flower.

No other part of the flower could sustain the tiny creature, so it goes to great lengths to find the life-giving nectar.

Like those flowers, every person we meet will have at least one redeeming quality. It just depends how hard we try to find it. Let's resolve to be like the hummingbird and dig deep to find the sweetness in everyone's character.

Tuesday — *April 26*

CONSTANT kindness can accomplish much. As the sun makes ice melt, kindness causes misunderstanding, mistrust and hostility to evaporate.   Albert Schweitzer.

Wednesday — *April 27*

THERE'S a story told of a storm in the early nineteenth century. Engineers feared that the river, swollen with all the extra rain, might wash away a railway bridge, so they drove an engine and several railway carriages on to it and left them there. The extra weight kept the bridge safely in place.

We might complain about the burden of our responsibilities at times, but sometimes what we see as burdens are, in fact, supports that keep us where we are meant to be. Just like that bridge, the extra weight is what makes us stronger.

Thursday — **April 28**

SOME people seem to radiate energy and enthusiasm whatever their age. The youth in their hearts eclipses whatever wrinkles may be on their faces.

Emily Dickinson must have had this in mind when she wrote, "We turn not older with years, but newer every day."

Words to keep in mind, whatever our age.

Friday — **April 29**

WHAT do you expect to see on wedding invitations? Perhaps ribbons, bells, hearts . . . However, our friend Rachel opted for something different — her wedding stationery had little frogs adorning the edges.

I was puzzled at first but soon everything was explained. Rachel and Gary are as romantic as the next couple, but going into the grandest adventure of their lives, they wanted to depend on something much closer to their heart.

Hearts and flowers are fine but these cute little creatures let everyone know that this happy couple *Fully Rely On God*.

Saturday — **April 30**

NEXT time you feel that things just aren't going your way, remember these literally uplifting words from inventor Henry Ford:

"When everything seems to be going against you, remember, the airplane takes off against the wind, not with it!"

May

Sunday — **May 1**

WORLD Laughter Day takes place on the first Sunday of May. Thousands of people gather worldwide to laugh together.

World Laughter Day was created by Dr Madan Kataria, founder of the worldwide Laughter Yoga movement. This celebration is intended to promote world peace and a global consciousness of togetherness and friendship. More than five thousand Laughter Clubs exist worldwide.

The first World Laughter Day gathering took place in Mumbai in 1995. There, twelve thousand members from local and international Laughter Clubs joined together in a massive laughter session.

"Happy-demic" was the first World Laughter Day gathering outside India in the year 2000 held in Copenhagen; it attracted more than ten thousand people. This event even merited a mention in the Guinness Book Of World Records.

As it says in Genesis 21:6, "Sarah said, 'God has brought me laughter and everyone who hears about this will laugh with me'."

Monday — **May 2**

OUR old friend Mary spotted these pearls of wisdom outside a church: *If you can't sleep, don't count sheep — talk to the Shepherd!*

Tuesday — *May 3*

GODMOTHER

WHAT would I give to a baby brand new?
  A gift to endure, that would last a life
    through?
There's one thing I'd offer I certainly know:
A talent for Wonder is what I'd bestow,
Bright eyes to see magic wherever they gaze
And ears to hear music, and mouth to give praise,
A mind full of marvels, alert and aware,
A heart overflowing with gladness and prayer.

Margaret Ingall.

Wednesday — *May 4*

THOSE who do good deeds know that there's nothing like them for brightening the day — and the world! Like everything else, though, good deeds come in various guises, and my favourites are the anonymous ones.

The author Thomas Carlyle would, I think, have agreed. After all, it was he who wrote, "The work an unknown good man has done is like a vein of water flowing hidden underground, secretly making the ground green."

Thursday — *May 5*

HERE are some words of wisdom seen on a poster in a university hall of residence — *Don't let your studies interfere with your education.*

And from our old friend Anon comes this thought: "If you're afraid to go too far, you will never go far enough."

WILD AND WONDERFUL

Friday — **May 6**

WHEN we look for wise words we usually turn to classic literature or the writings of ancient philosophers, not necessarily the Internet.

But that's where Pam found these thought-provoking words. She could not see an author, but these modern words seem to have a lot of old-fashioned faith behind them.

It will be all right in the end. If it's not right, then it's not the end!

Saturday — **May 7**

THERE may well be scientific proof behind this claim. Well, I doubt it, but that doesn't stop me from thinking it's an experiment we should all take part in.

"Sunshine is good for your teeth. So smile!"

Sunday — **May 8**

HAVE you ever thought how wonderful our alphabet is? Twenty-six letters can be arranged one way to make us cry, another way to make us smile. Arrange them yet again and you can encapsulate the depths, the heights and the history of human endeavour.

Nothing else encompasses so much for us – except Jesus. Perhaps that's why He used the Greek alphabet to describe Himself when He promised to be everything for us!

"I am the Alpha and Omega, the beginning and the ending, saith the Lord, which is, and which was, and which is to come, the Almighty."

(Revelation 1:8)

Monday — *May 9*

ALICE'S local primary school has a garden for the children, and is always grateful for adult volunteers. It took Alice some time to decide to offer her services, but it's now her favourite part of the week.

"There's nothing like seeing the children's faces as they watch the plants grow and produce fruit," she smiled. "It really does remind me that life is full of marvels that most of us never notice. I just wish I'd started helping long ago."

As E. Merrill Root once observed, "We need a renaissance of wonder. We need to renew in our hearts and in our souls, the deathless dream, the eternal poetry, the perennial sense that life is miracle and magic."

For it is, you know!

Tuesday — *May 10*

WHEN it comes to looking for the advantages of advancing years, we rarely have to look far. When we are young we are seldom the masters of our fate, being pulled this way and that by the challenges of life, trying to make our way in the world.

But when we advance down that path of life a little, we tend to gain more freedom along the way.

Veteran actress, Shirley MacLaine, put it like this: "I think of life now as a wonderful play I have written for myself. And so my purpose is to have the utmost fun playing my part!"

Play on. You deserve it!

Wednesday — *May 11*

WHEN is the perfect time to be happy? Well, maybe after that unexpected bill is sorted out, or after a friend who has been ill starts to feel better, or after the Spring cleaning is done.

The point is, there's always something, or so it seems, to get in the way. That's why I'm grateful for these encouraging words:

"Happiness doesn't lie in waiting for the storm to pass. It lies in getting out there and learning to dance in the rain."

Thursday — *May 12*

IT has to be admitted — angels can be very elusive and that's why I like these thoughts on the subject.

"The guardian angels of life fly so high as to be beyond our sight, but they are always looking down upon us." Jean Paul Richter.

"If trouble hearing Angel song with thine ears, try listening with thy heart." Meriel Stellinger.

And, particularly reassuring is this thought:

"Angels are never too distant to hear you."

Friday — *May 13*

SURELY everything gets thinner as it's spread out further? And surely everything wears out the more it's used?

Everything? Well, that's not quite true. There is one thing that seems to defy all such laws, as Victor Hugo explains:

"Maternal love. A miraculous substance which God multiplies as he divides it."

CROATIAN CALM

Saturday — **May 14**

*A*S for Rosemarine (rosemary), I let it runne all over my garden walls, not onlie because my bees love it, but because it is the herb sacred to remembrance, and therefore to friendship.

These are the words of Sir Thomas More (1478-1535). Born in London, he was an able lawyer, a man of principle, piety and of great learning. He was concerned with the social troubles of his time, and wrote this in his book "Utopia":

"There are many things in the commonwealth of Utopia that I rather wish than hope to see, adopted in our own." The word Utopia comes from the Greek meaning nowhere, and is now part of our everyday language, meaning an imaginary place where everything is perfect.

Let us all aspire to work towards perfection today — and every day.

Sunday — **May 15**

THEY may have been separated by centuries and continents, but I think Lloyd John Ogilvie and Robert Louis Stevenson would have understood each other well.

Ogilvie, Chaplain of the United States Senate, said, "The secret of life is that all we have and are is a gift of grace to be shared."

While Robert Louis Stevenson, that great man of letters, wrote: "There is nothing but God's grace. We walk upon it; we breathe it; it makes the nails and axles of the universe."

"From the fullness of His grace we have all received one blessing after another."   (John 1:16)

Monday — *May 16*

HERE is a thought-provoking quote from the pen of Henry David Thoreau:

"The true harvest of my daily life is somewhat as intangible and indescribable as the tints of morning or evening. It is a little star-dust caught, a segment of the rainbow which I have clutched."

Something worthwhile to contemplate at the start — or indeed the end — of the day, don't you think?

Tuesday — *May 17*

"I DON'T want to grow old," a wise woman once told her grandchildren. "I don't mind growing older, but I don't want to grow old."

She often liked to join in their less energetic games but didn't often run about with them. Instead she watched them, laughed with them and encouraged them. What a good way to join in and to keep young!

This reminds me of the truth in these words: "We don't stop playing because we grow old; we grow old because we stop playing."

Wednesday — *May 18*

A PROSPECTOR deep in the Brazilian jungle was explaining to a village headman why gold and silver were so precious.

The headman listened carefully and then said, "We also love gold and silver — the golden sun and the silver moon. We need no other."

The prospector went home, a humbler and wiser man.

Thursday — *May 19*

HAVE you heard of Friendship Bread? Well, it starts with a cup of yeast. The sugar, flour and yeast make it rise until you have about four cups of "starter".

One cup goes towards baking a loaf, two cups should go to friends so they can share in the experience and pass it on to their friends who would, in turn, pass it on to their friends.

And the fourth cup? Well, it begins the next cycle of friendship.

Life would be impossible without our "daily bread" and extremely unhappy without friends, so anything that combines the two just has to be a recipe for success.

Friday — *May 20*

HAVING experienced kindness and love, don't you wonder why some folk seem to struggle so hard to accept them? When you enjoy the wonderful benefits that come from caring for another person, you might be excused for thinking that kindness to others was almost a selfish act.

Rose Pastor Stokes, a nineteenth-century Russian émigré, summed it up well when she wrote: "Fill the cup of happiness for others and there will be enough overflowing to fill yours to the brim!"

Saturday — *May 21*

THE key to being the best friend possible might be found in this definition from Arnold Glasow: "A friend never gets in your way – unless you happen to be going down."

Sunday — *May 22*

JOHN 10:10

*L*IFE in abundance; life to the full
This is the promise made to us all.
No buts or exceptions,
  This pledge is sincere
A gift from our Father,
  Who holds us most dear,
Rejoice in His goodness,
  Give thanks to above
And share with your fellows
  the fruits of His love.

M. J. Brison.

Monday — *May 23*

HAVE you ever heard the proverb: *Bloom where you are planted*? When Beverley moved to a different city it was a difficult adjustment for her. She missed her friends and familiar surroundings.

So, one day, a group of her old friends visited her and brought along an enormous pot of bright yellow chrysanthemums.

"Oh!" she exclaimed, as she opened the door of her new home. "Are those for me?"

"Yes, they are," came the reply. "They're a daily reminder."

Beverley was puzzled until her former neighbour Chris recited the little proverb and explained the flowers were a wonderful way to remember that in all circumstances we can choose to radiate brightness and beauty.

Beverley's blooms flourished in her front porch, bringing cheer to everyone on her street. And so did she!

Tuesday — *May 24*

SOME people disregard humility as a quality, but did you know that the word "humble" and the word "human" come from the same root? Both are derived from "humus", in other words, "earth".

Whenever we are tempted to get too big for our boots let's remember where we came from. And who made it happen.

Wednesday — *May 25*

I ENJOY reading about other cultures. They help us see that while our everyday lives might be quite different, the things that matter most are the same the world over.

This beautiful saying from Madagascar uses the natural world to paint an image we can all identify with: "Let your love be like the misty rains, coming softly but flooding the river."

Thursday — *May 26*

SAINTS are not born — they begin life as ordinary men and women with human frailties which they learn to overcome. Augustine of Hippo lived a life of drunkenness and dishonesty, rebelling against every rule his devout mother laid down.

However, after finding faith he turned his life around and St Augustine's Day is still celebrated on 26th May, many centuries after his death.

Augustine himself described his journey in a way we can all relate to. In his Confessions he wrote, "You made us for yourself, O God, and our hearts are restless — until they rest in you."

Friday — **May 27**

WHENEVER I read articles about wealth, I like to keep in mind these uplifting words from Henry Ward Beecher:

"No man can tell whether he is rich or poor by turning to his ledger. It is the heart that makes a man rich. He is rich according to what he is, not according to what he has."

Saturday — **May 28**

WHEN a kindness you sowed
    Blooms into a thousand colours,
        Pick a star.
When a challenge crumbles
    Beneath your courage,
        Pick a star.
When success suddenly shows up
And sits down beside you,
        Pick a star.
When night draws its drapes
And your day has been lived with
Honesty, love and gentleness,
        Pick a star.
        Reach high,
    As high as you can,
        Past the sun,
        Past the moon
    And pick a star —
The biggest and brightest you can find.
    Fasten it in your hair,
    Put it in your pocket,
    Wear it on your finger
        And celebrate!
                            Rachel Wallace–Oberle.

Sunday — *May 29*

TENNIS star Serena Williams is famous for her athletic prowess, for the Grand Slam titles she has won, and for having been the number one female tennis player in the world. And there's another equally impressive, but perhaps not so well known, fact about her.

In most of her changeovers, she would lower her head, close her eyes and say a silent prayer. Not for victory, but to stay strong, whether she was destined to win or lose.

"Surely God is my salvation; I will trust him and not be afraid. The Lord, the Lord, is my strength and my song; he has become my salvation."

(Isaiah 12:2)

Monday — *May 30*

IT'S not that long since street lights came to one of the remote islands in the Outer Hebrides of Scotland. Local folk were generally glad to have the extra brightness, but one man missed seeing the stars.

"Who took away my night sky?" he was heard to ask. Sometimes we don't notice what's precious until it's too late.

Tuesday — *May 31*

I'M sure we all want to make things better for others, but we don't always have the resources. Well, perhaps we could look at it in a different way.

As our friend John suggested, "If you can't be the pencil that writes someone happiness, then try to be the eraser that rubs out some of their sorrows."

June

Wednesday — **June 1**

A GARDEN is a place to be nurtured and enjoyed — when a gardener's work is over it is time to take a well-earned rest, a sentiment expressed to perfection in this gardener's prayer.

O Lord, please listen to my prayer
As I sit upon my garden chair.
I've cut the hedge and mowed the lawn
And planted seeds from early morn.
So now I pray you, make them grow
Like the pictures on the packets show.
We'd all like to say *Amen* to that!

Thursday — **June 2**

WE'VE all seen pictures of the Empire State Building, dominating the New York skyline. When it was completed it was the tallest building in the world and it has been named as one of the Wonders of the Modern World and designated a National Landmark.

The builders could not have guessed how iconic the building would become — but they did know there was a worldwide economic slump when they started its construction and the United States was in the grip of the Great Depression.

For me the Empire State Building stands as an enduring promise that even from the worst of times, something wonderful can arise!

Friday — **June 3**

I HAVE read that when translators were working on a Bible for the Inuit peoples they hit on an ingenious way of communicating a verse on repentance. That verse is about the joy of the angels in heaven over one sinner who repents.

The greatest sign of joy the Inuit knew was the wagging of their dogs' tails, so the verse literally says in Inuit "great was the wagging of angels' tails"! What a perfect solution.

Saturday — **June 4**

HERE are some reflective words written by William Arthur Ward: "A true friend knows your weaknesses but shows you your strengths; feels your fears but fortifies your faith; sees your anxieties but frees your spirit; recognises your disabilities but emphasises your possibilities."

Sunday — **June 5**

A TRAVELLER was unpacking in a hotel. Opening his suitcase he dropped the small padlock he had secured it with. The padlock bounced off the toe of his shoe and rolled under the bed.

As he reached down, the traveller noticed a card on the carpet. It lay under the middle of the bed and it said, *Yes, we even clean here*!

Works of faith should be like that, found in the darkest reaches, where no-one expects them to be.

"But I tell you who hear me: Love your enemies, do good to those who hate you, bless those who curse you, pray for those who mistreat you."

(Luke 6:27-28)

Monday — *June 6*

IRISES are, in their rainbow of colours, one of the glories of early Summer gardens.

In classical mythology Iris was portrayed as young and beautiful, the rainbow goddess, who restored the peace of Nature and was a mediator. It was said that rainbows were the paths of Iris's feet when she acted as the messenger of the goddesses.

Juno, whose chariot was pulled by peacocks, is believed by some to have given her name to June, the month when many irises bloom in their glorious shades of lilac, blue, apricot, yellow and white.

Tuesday — *June 7*

WHEN all the woes of the world were released from it, the last thing left in Pandora's box, according to legend, was Hope. It seems such a gentle thing, but often it's what sustains us until the sun rises and our fortunes improve again.

Emily Dickinson summed it up well when she wrote:

"Hope" is the thing with feathers
That perches in the soul
And sings the tune without the words
And never stops at all.

Wednesday — *June 8*

ONE day not long ago I saw this acronym for Bible that made me smile: *Basic Information Before Leaving Earth.*

Something to think about, indeed!

SUMMER SCENTS

Thursday — **June 9**

I SAW it through the window
  When waking up this morn,
Wrapped in glowing colours was
  A brand-new shining dawn.
Before I'd done admiring,
  Time peeled it all away,
To show a gentle morning
  With sky of palest grey,
But then a silver shower
  Dissolved the cloud cocoon,
Revealing — yes, a butterfly
  Of golden afternoon.
I basked within its sunshine
  Till evening's fading light
Disclosed yet further treasure:
  A velvet, star-filled night.
No gift could be more lovely
  Than this enchanted day,
But wait — I hear another one's
  Already on its way!

Margaret Ingall.

Friday — **June 10**

"SHE will pull through," a friend said to the Lady of the House. "She's a survivor." She was speaking about Elspeth who has had a few setbacks in her life and had just met with another.

She always gets over them and I know how she succeeds. She sets aside a few minutes every day to sit alone in silence and think of all she has to be grateful for: her friends, her home, her health.

Simple, but it works for Elspeth, and it could work well for you, too.

Saturday — **June 11**

MANNERS. Those of us who have children and grandchildren know how difficult they can be to teach, but when we see them flower in the next generation we realise why we tried so hard.

As Erastus Wiman, a nineteenth-century writer and businessman, pointed out, "Nothing is ever lost by courtesy. It is the cheapest of pleasure, costs nothing and conveys much."

Sunday — **June 12**

OUR old friend Mary told me that she cherishes this Daily Acceptance Prayer which has often given her great peace of mind:

I accept myself completely.
I accept my strengths and my weaknesses,
My gifts and my shortcomings,
My good points and my faults.

I accept myself completely as a human being.
I accept that I am here to learn and grow, and
I accept that I am learning and growing.
I accept the personality I've developed, and
I accept my power to heal and change.

I accept myself without condition or reservation.
I accept that the core of my being is goodness
And that my essence is love, and
I accept that I sometimes forget that.

I accept my own life as a blessing and a gift.
My heart is open to receive, and I am deeply
grateful.
May I always share the gifts that I receive
Fully, freely, and with joy.

Monday — **June 13**

DO you ever stop and just give thanks for the wonders that surround us, even on what you might call an "average" day?

Izaak Walton, seventeenth-century poet and author of "The Compleat Angler", put it this way:

"The sun in its full glory, either at rising or setting – this and many other like blessings we enjoy daily. And for most of them, because they are so common, most forget to pay their praises. But let not us."

Tuesday — **June 14**

OUR friend Norah likes these quotes by Norman Vincent Peale and I hope that you'll enjoy sharing them today:

"Empty pockets never held anyone back. Only empty heads and empty hearts can do that."

"Imagination is the true magic carpet."

"It's always too early to quit."

Wednesday — **June 15**

ROBERT Randolph is a funk and soul Christian rocker. He was voted amongst "Rolling Stone" magazine's one hundred greatest guitarists ever and has toured with Eric Clapton.

When asked about the lyrical content of his songs he said, "When I wake up in the morning, I want my friends, family and fans to know what I believe in and what I'm all about. That's what should be important."

Let's decide what really matters to us, then live each day in such a way that people we meet know exactly what we are all about.

Thursday — **June 16**

I HAVE heard there are Native Americans whose families have long been making the most beautiful pottery. It is made from traditional local clay and they are helped by their ancestors.

How? Well, the older folk search the ground for broken pieces of ancient pottery that lie scattered in the area. They pound them into a powder and mix it with the new clay.

We would call it recycling but for these folk the practice has a deeper meaning as the handiwork of their forebears combines with their own skills to produce objects of beauty for the next generation.

Friday — **June 17**

WHEN I asked a nurse what was the best thing she could do to comfort a patient she answered without hesitation, "Hold their hand."

It's true, isn't it? You can say so much with your hands. To the sick it says, "Hold on. I am with you."

To a close friend your handshake says, "It's good to see you again," while to the stranger it says, "Welcome, I'm pleased to meet you."

A hand can be a greeting or a wave of goodbye. It can say thank you, good luck and deliver a whole host of other messages. In truth, you can often say more with your hand than with any words.

Saturday — **June 18**

SAMUEL Goldwyn, the legendary film producer, knew more than most about applause.

"When someone does something good," he said, "Applaud. You will make two people happy."

Sunday — *June 19*

OWN up all of you who have experienced occasions when you have felt that life just wasn't being fair. Quite a few of you, I'm sure.

Certainly George Matheson would have had more reason than most to feel that way when, as a young man studying for the ministry, not only did his eyesight begin to fail, but his fiancée left him, unable to cope with the thought of being married to a blind man. Nor did his disability do anything to help his longed-for career as a church leader.

In spite of all his sufferings, he was still able to write a hymn which was to bring comfort to so many, "Oh Love That Will Not Let Me Go":

O joy that seekest me from pain,
I cannot close my heart to thee:
I trace the rainbow through the rain,
And feel the promise is not vain,
That morn shall tearless be.

Small wonder that George Matheson went on to find much fulfilment and success in pastoral ministry, for his words are a wonderful reminder that even when we may feel tempted to give up, God will never give up on us.

Monday — *June 20*

SOMETIMES words of wisdom can work on many different levels. Consider these from the author William A. Ward. They made me smile, they made me think. And they also made me stand up straight and point my toes!

"A well developed sense of humour is the pole that adds balance to your steps, as you walk the tightrope of life."

Tuesday — **June 21**

JOHN Ruskin, the Victorian designer and art critic, was a guest at a social event. His hostess accidentally spotted her prized silk handkerchief with ink. Seeing how distraught she was, Ruskin retired to the next room and returned having penned an exquisite design around the blot.

No life is without its "blots" and there is nothing we can do about that. What we can do, however, is to choose to take those situations and make them better. And sometimes, like Mr Ruskin, we can even make them beautiful!

Wednesday — **June 22**

PRAYER OF MY HEART

LORD, please remodel and refurnish my heart.
Raise the ceiling in Faith's room so it can
stretch and grow.
Add tall windows in Peace's room so it can
stream out to shine on others.
Construct balconies in Joy's room so it can dance
their length, clearly visible to all.
Build a basement in Love's room so it will
become deeper, stronger and unconditional.
Knock out walls and tear out floors in Gratitude's
room so it will pour out like a river.
Light a lamp and add a sofa in Grace's room so
all who come will want to stay.
May every room in my heart be decorated with
a new song for you, Lord.
Amen.

Rachel Wallace-Oberle.

Thursday — **June 23**

"**H**OW many people die from snake bites every year?" asked our friend John. I thought carefully but couldn't come up with an answer.

"None," he replied. "They die from the poison!"

He had the last laugh – but it gave me food for thought. I have met people who have harboured resentments over trivial matters and long after the deed itself is forgotten, relationships have suffered.

However, we don't need to let that happen. Like any intrepid explorer, we will be bitten from time to time, bitten by words, looks and accusations. But if we don't take on board the poison of resentment, then those "snakes" lose their power and are soon forgotten.

And without the snakes the jungle of life is a much nicer place!

Friday — **June 24**

USUALLY the Beatitudes refer to the Sermon on the Mount. Our friend Pat was observing a bumble-bee in her flower beds one sunny day when she came up with some "Bee-attitudes."

The secret of the little creature's happiness, it seemed, lay in the following, and these are good thoughts for all of us to keep in mind, too:

Bee busy – *doing what you love to do.*
Bee true – *to the dreams God has for you.*
Bee sure – *to taste the sweetness of the day.*
Bee silly – *laugh lots and take time off to play.*
Bee bold – *enough to trust your wings and fly.*
Bee-lieve – *the power of prayer will get you by.*
Bee happy – *keep your outlook bright and sunny.*
Bee yourself – *because you really are a honey!*

BLUE HORIZON

Saturday — *June 25*

I WAS surprised to see the same word — *Damayan* — applied to a television show, a migrant workers' association, and a garden project showing people how to grow fresh vegetables in inner city gardens.

Damayan, a Filipino word, is defined as either, "working together for mutual healing", "helping each other", or "treating another person's hunger as your own".

So, no single definition then, but I soon realised it didn't really matter. No matter which meaning we consider, wouldn't we all be better off with a little *Damayan* in our lives?

Sunday — *June 26*

WHY did "sea hearts" fascinate both Christopher Columbus and Benjamin Franklin?

Well, these large, shiny, shelled beans fall from trees, float down rivers and can even drift across oceans — sometimes for many years — before finding land, putting down roots and growing. Legend has it that Columbus wanted to find where the sea hearts came from and Benjamin Franklin used them to plot the Gulf Stream.

Most of their existence is spent seemingly without purpose, merely drifting, but at a time and place not decided by them, they come ashore and new life blossoms. Our lives have a purpose, too, whether we are aware of it or not. Like the sea heart we float on God's tide, waiting until He needs us to come ashore.

"You are the God of my salvation: on you I will wait all the day." (Psalm 25:5)

Monday — **June 27**

THERE are few sunny days that Anna doesn't spend working hard in her garden, toiling away at any of the hundred and one jobs that always need doing. So on a perfect June afternoon I caught sight of her sitting back relaxing in a deckchair.

"I *am* busy," she laughed, as she saw me. "I'm busy relaxing! And here's a quote for you, Francis — it's the reason why I'm sitting here right now. It's from John Lubbock, who was a politician and also a biologist.

"He said, 'Rest is not idleness, and to lie sometimes on the grass under the trees on a Summer's day, listening to the murmur of water, or watching the clouds float across the sky, is by no means a waste of time.'"

Some of the best horticultural advice I've ever heard!

Tuesday — **June 28**

THERE'S an old piece of folk wisdom which states: "If the first thing you do each day is eat a frog, then nothing worse will happen for the rest of the day."

I'm not sure I would recommend this idea but I think I understand. If there's something unpleasant to be done, and you don't do it then it will sit beside you all day, becoming less and less appealing as time goes by. But if you get it over and done with as soon as you can, then the rest of the day is a breeze in comparison.

So, if you want to enjoy the day instead of spending it worrying, then go on, eat that frog!

THE FRIENDSHIP BOOK

Wednesday — *June 29*

WHEN Gillian came into a small windfall, her first action was to invite all her friends to accompany her on a day-trip to the seaside.

"I suppose I could have bought myself a nice present," she said. "But the pleasure of that would have soon faded, whereas I'll always cherish the fun and pleasure of sharing a day out with my friends."

As James Joyce once observed: "While you have a thing it can be taken from you, but when you give it, you have given it. No robber can take it from you. It is yours then for ever when you have given it. It will be yours always."

And love and friendship really are worth keeping — always.

Thursday — *June 30*

IRVING Berlin composed such musical classics as "Let's Face The Music And Dance", "Puttin' On The Ritz" and the much-loved "I'm Dreaming Of A White Christmas".

When an interviewer, tired of the same old questions, asked him what he would like to be asked, he said, "Ask me how I feel about the many songs I've written that *didn't* become hits."

The interviewer duly obliged and Berlin responded, "I still think they are wonderful!"

Some of his songs made the world come alive for so many, but he cared just as much for those that nobody had noticed. If a composer could feel that way about his creations, who can doubt that the least of us are loved as much as the greatest by Someone who is always there?

SUNNY SKETCHES

July

REJOICING in the Summer sun
  The busy bumble bees,
Bright butterflies go flitting by,
  There's birdsong in the trees.
The kingfisher, a flash of blue,
  Dives swiftly to the stream,
And Summer magic touches hearts
  As softly as a dream.

A colony of busy ants
  Is rushing here and there,
Industrious and organised,
  We simply stand and stare.
These golden days flow gently by,
  The year is in its prime,
And all of nature celebrates
  The joy of Summertime.

                              Iris Hesselden.

AT this time of year many of us will be avidly watching Wimbledon. Top players, at the peak of their abilities, play with style and sportsmanship.

Our old friend Mary will be watching as usual this year, but uppermost in her mind will be these words of wisdom passed on by her friend Irene:

"You'll find life is very like a game of tennis," she said. "The one who serves best usually wins."

Sunday — *July 3*

MOST of us know the twenty-third Psalm but here's a new take on the well-loved verses.

The Lord is my Shepherd — That's relationship!
I shall not want — That's supply!
He makes me lie down in green pastures —
*   That's rest!*
He leads me beside still waters —
*   That's refreshment!*
He restores my soul — That's healing!
He leads me in the paths of righteousness —
*   That's guidance!*
For His name's sake — That's purpose!
Yea, though I walk through the valley of the
*   shadow of death — That's testing!*
I will fear no evil — That's protection!
For you are with me — That's faithfulness!
Your rod and staff comfort me — That's discipline!
You prepare a table before me in the presence of
*   my enemies — That's hope!*
You anoint my head with oil — That's consecration!
My cup runs over — That's abundance!
Surely goodness and mercy shall follow me all the
*   days of my life — That's blessing!*
And I will dwell in the house of the Lord —
*   That's security!*
Forever — That's eternity!

Monday — *July 4*

RALPH Waldo Emerson had this to say of friendships:

"When they are real, they are not glass threads or frost-work, but the solidest thing we know."

How true these words are.

Tuesday — *July 5*

THE kindness shown by people never ceases to astound me and should, I think, be considered amongst the wonders of this world.

I am reminded of a woman who didn't hesitate to move her three nephews in with her own family after they became homeless. The fact that she and her husband barely made ends meet before didn't seem to be a problem.

The Danes have an apt saying for times like this: "Where there is room in the heart — there is room in the house."

Wednesday — *July 6*

I AM guessing that the author of this proverb was not only wise, but was also rich and content in his or her anonymity.

"Contentment is the philosopher's stone which turns all it touches into gold. The rich man is poor without it, the poor man rich with it."

Thursday — *July 7*

WILL ROGERS, the famous actor, had these words of advice for people feeling just that bit older:

"Whenever you wish you were young again — remember algebra!"

In other words every age has drawbacks as well as advantages. In a more thoughtful mood he described our "September years" in these memorable words:

"One must wait until evening to see how splendid the day has been."

Friday — **July 8**

LISA wasn't anyone famous. Homeless, she sold "The Big Issue" in Dundee, first on a draughty footbridge, then outside the railway station.

When, aged twenty-five, she died of pneumonia, you might not think anyone would take much notice but you would be quite wrong. It turned out that her cheerful smile had won many friends.

People remembered how she would hurry to help them from a taxi, even carry their bags for them. And although she had many troubles of her own, she was always ready to listen to those of others.

Lisa was no angel and she didn't pretend to be. However, there was standing room only at her funeral service, because so many folk wanted to pay their respects to the little woman with the big smile.

Saturday — **July 9**

DOREEN was laughing as she explained how, as a small girl, she was the despair of her brother when it came to catching a ball.

"He so often used to call me butterfingers," she said, "that I'll now have great pleasure in showing him this quote by Ed Pudol: 'When blessing comes into your hands, don't forget to share with others, so that blessing will not stop in your hands. Let the blessings spread and flow from your hands infinitely.'

"So, you see, it is all right not to hang on to whatever lands in your fingers!"

And as Doreen's generosity is well known, I didn't doubt that this time her brother will agree!

Sunday — *July 10*

ROSEMARY was about to move into a smaller house and, like anyone who's ever been through that experience, was finding it hard to decide what to take and what to leave behind.

"But then I began to realise," she told me, "that the more I gave away or discarded, the more liberated I felt. I suppose it's a bit like life itself. We hold on to so many old attitudes, old grudges, old fears, just because it's become a habit.

"It's not until we decide to move on that we realise how much lighter we feel without those burdens. There's a lot to be said for travelling light, and I intend to do my best to."

As Rosemary has found out, these words from Ecclesiastes 3:6 are relevant; there is indeed "a time to get, and a time to lose; a time to keep and a time to cast away".

Monday — *July 11*

IN Chinese tradition, harp strings have long been a symbol of friendship. It stems from a story of a skilled harp player and a skilled listener.

When the harpist played music from the mountains, the listener would proclaim he could practically see the hill before him. When the harpist played water music, the listener sighed and said he could feel the crystal stream flowing around his feet. However, when the listener died the harpist cut his strings and never played again.

We don't all get to play beautiful music in this life, but the music is only half the story. As the harpist found out, it's the skilled listener who makes it all worthwhile!

Tuesday — *July 12*

SAM had always been a perfectionist and often found it difficult to move beyond his mistakes and failures. Then he came across these words by author Jack Kornfield: "If your compassion does not include yourself, it is incomplete."

Sam now tries to approach each day with grace, not only for others, but also for himself and seems much happier and relaxed. We could all benefit from such an attitude, don't you agree?

Wednesday — *July 13*

THIS is one of the most fascinating facts from the space programme. Accelerating takes the Space Shuttle into a higher, slower, orbit around the Earth, while decelerating causes the shuttle to fall into a tighter, faster orbit. So slowing down actually makes it go faster!

In a way it's the same with family life. When our lives are "full speed ahead" our relationships slow down. But when we put our foot on the brake, slowing down, we actually get far more of the important stuff done.

Perhaps that's why grandparents are so "out of this world" when it comes to families!

Thursday — *July 14*

NOBODY likes setbacks or difficult times, but how would we learn and grow without them?

Louisa May Alcott, author of "Little Women", summed it up well when she wrote: "I am not afraid of storms, for I am learning to sail my ship!"

Friday — **July 15**

*G*IVE me a garden
 With a bit of sun,
And I will not rest
 Until the work is done.
Give me a garden
 With a bit of wind,
And I will endure
 To bring the harvest in.
Give me a garden
 With a bit of rain,
And I will believe
 That fortitude remains.
Give me a garden,
 Just a little earth,
And I will become
 Someone of great worth.

Rachel Wallace-Oberle.

Saturday — **July 16**

IT'S rarely that we have no regrets in life. While most of us live the best way we can, almost everyone has something they would change.

Perhaps they would have been kinder to someone, perhaps they wouldn't have said the words that caused that difference of opinion or maybe they would have eaten fewer cakes and sweet treats, looked after their figure — and teeth!

The "what ifs" would be different for each of us, but we can all take advantage of these words:

"Though no-one can go back and make a brand-new start, anyone can start from now and make a brand-new ending."

PERFECT PARTNERS

Sunday — **July 17**

WE can all be nice to friends and loved ones, but it takes extra courage to love someone we don't like. In the Hitopadesha, a collection of Sanskrit fables, the author tells us:

"Hospitality is to be shown, even to an enemy. The tree doth not withdraw its shade, even from the woodcutter."

And the Bible says: "You have heard that it was said, 'Love your neighbour and hate your enemy'. But I tell you: Love your enemies and pray for those who persecute you."   (Matthew 5:43-44)

Monday — **July 18**

WILLIAM Warfield, the baritone who starred in a stage version of "Porgy And Bess" and sang "Ole Man River" in MGM's colour version of "Showboat", had more than his fair share of difficulties in life, not the least of which were problems with his voice. But this inspirational man had his own take on hard times.

"When the rungs were missing on the ladder," he said, "Well, that's when I learned to leap!"

Tuesday — **July 19**

WHEN Clara travelled to the Holy Land a few years ago, she returned with these words jotted down among her souvenirs and photographs. Seen on a wall inscription on her travels, she says that they inspire her every day to look beyond what she can see:

I believe in the sun even when it is not shining.
I believe in love even when not feeling it.
I believe in God even when He is silent.

Wednesday — *July 20*

FAMOUS photographer David Bailey once said, "In photography everything is ordinary. It takes a lot of looking before you learn to see the extraordinary."

But once you learn how to look, you find it everywhere.

Perhaps surprisingly, rocker Jon Bon Jovi has a similar attitude to miracles. "Change your perception of what a miracle is," he said, "and you'll see them all around you."

Whether we are searching for a great picture or a miracle, it seems they are out there. All we have to do is look.

Thursday — *July 21*

SING a song and let your gladness
Float from windows, fly through doors,
Let it touch your friends and neighbours,
Lifting hearts to sing like yours.
Let each note swell ever louder
Spreading sweetness o'er the land,
Helping all who hear its music
Feel the song and understand
Life with all its joys and sorrows
Carries still a value rare
So unite in joyful music
Let your singing fill the air!
Margaret Ingall.

Friday — *July 22*

BETTER than a thousand hollow words is one word that brings peace. Buddha.

Saturday — *July 23*

A WATER fountain can just be an ornamental addition to a garden, or it may give vital nourishment and life to the plants growing around it. But what about a "fountain of gladness" — what's that?

Well, author Washington Irving may not have been a gardener, but he certainly knew people. "A kind heart," he informs us, "is a fountain of gladness, making everything in its vicinity freshen into smiles."

Sunday — *July 24*

HOW do you cope with setbacks? Do you tend to adopt a "Woe is me" attitude, or do you try to see adversity as part of a bigger plan?

Explorer Samuel Hearne was at the beginning of a major expedition in northern Canada when thieves stole most of his supplies. In his diary he wrote: "The weight of our baggage being lightened, our next day's journey was more swift and pleasant."

Then Jesus said to his disciples: "Therefore I tell you, do not worry about your life, what you will eat or drink; or about your body, what you will wear. Life is more than food and the body more than clothes." (Luke 12: 22-23)

Monday — *July 25*

HERE'S an interesting play on words I recently saw on a sign outside a church: *Patience is a virtue that carries a lot of wait.* How true!

Tuesday — **July 26**

IF you could have anything in the world, what would it be? It's an enticing thought, without doubt. But let me suggest a simple answer that comes to us across the centuries from the Greek playwright, Euripides.

"It is a good thing to be rich," he wrote, "and it is a good thing to be strong, but it is a better thing to be beloved of many friends."

Now, if you could wish for anything could you wish for anything better? And if you already are "beloved of many friends", I'm sure you'll agree that nothing else is needed!

Wednesday — **July 27**

PERHAPS you have never really thought of yourself as the brave explorer type? Then think about these words from an anonymous author:

"There is goodness in everything. Our job is to find it. In every setback there is the key to success. Our challenge is to find it. In every person, the best is there. It's up to us to discover it!"

Treasure hunting, anyone?

Thursday — **July 28**

HOW many of our worries are really too small to fret about when all is said and done? Corrie Ten Boom, survivor of the Holocaust and worker for reconciliation, knew worries big and small and had her own opinion on what to do with each.

"Any concern too small to be turned into a prayer," she wrote, "is certainly too small to be made into a burden."

Friday — **July 29**

THERE'S one star — the sun — that fills our days with light. There are other stars that are easy to pick out on a clear night but there are millions of stars shining equally brightly, only they are too far away for us to see.

Each day countless people help others without it making the news and as a Finnish proverb reminds us: "Even the smallest star helps light up the darkness!"

Saturday — **July 30**

IF we focus too much on life's grand events we might miss out on all the little moments in between. The nineteenth-century French writer Victor Cherbuliez reminds us: "Half of life's joy is in little things, taken on the run."

Sunday — **July 31**

THERE'S a sculpture on a Scottish sea-front which depicts a fishing boat and a huge approaching wave. The inscription is an old Breton prayer: *God, your sea is so great and my boat is so small.*

We might be great or small, powerful or weak but at one time or another we all need help. As the fishermen from Brittany recognised only too well, there is one defence we can all call on whatever the circumstances.

"He replied, 'You of little faith, why are you so afraid?' Then he got up and rebuked the wind and the waves and it was completely calm."

(Matthew 8: 26)

August

Monday — **August 1**

SIR John Lubbock was, I think, a very wise man — not only because he created Bank Holidays and gave us an extra few days' break, but because he justified them thus:

"Rest is not idleness, and to lie sometimes on the grass under trees on a Summer's day, listening to the murmur of water or watching the clouds float across the sky, is by no means a waste of time."

Thank you, Sir John.

Tuesday — **August 2**

ED LUCAS was a blind sports writer. As a boy in a school for the visually impaired he would sometimes complain about not being able to do things.

"We're all in the same boat here, Ed," his teacher would remind him. "So pick up your oar and start rowing."

We might not have Ed's difficulties with eyesight to overcome, but each step we take along life's road will inevitably have its own pitfalls. Just think about it for a moment. What might be an insurmountable problem to someone might be just the thing you can help with, and vice versa.

In a very real sense we are all in the same boat, travelling on the same journey, so let's pick up our oars and let's all start rowing — together.

Wednesday — *August 3*

WHY are some people more able than others to appreciate the good things in their lives? Perhaps it's the looking that does the trick.

Hymn writer Maltbie Babcock observed: "Be on the lookout for mercies. The more we look for them the more of them we will see. For blessings brighten when we count them!"

Thursday — *August 4*

THOMAS Jefferson certainly made his mark on the wider world. He was the third president of the United States and primary author of the Declaration of Independence, but he knew the real value of an "ordinary" life, when he wrote this:

"He does most in God's great world, who does his best in his own little world."

Friday — *August 5*

IF you have a sister, today is an occasion to celebrate – 5th August is Sisters' Day and there's surely no better time to pick up the phone, send a card or an e-mail, or visit your sibling to show how much you appreciate her.

Sisters' Day was established to strengthen a special bond, share precious memories and create new ones. A sister is someone you can call on no matter what, someone who always has time for you. Sometimes friends move on, but the relationship with a sister is forever.

As Isadora James said: "A sister is a gift to the heart, a friend to the spirit, a golden thread to the meaning of life."

*Saturday — **August 6***

A BUSY day with things to do
And people I must see,
And yet somehow I find the time
  For one more cup of tea.
And if the day's a dreary one
  No bright or cheery news,
A biscuit and a pot of tea
  Will chase away the blues.
Through happy times and troubled times,
  In laughter and in tears,
We put the kettle on once more
  And share the cup that cheers.
                    Iris Hesselden.

*Sunday — **August 7***

NOTRE Dame is without doubt the most
magnificent of Parisian cathedrals, but many
think the church of Sacré Coeur is just as beautiful,
in a different way.

Approaching this building you find two paths in
front of you; one circles around, allowing for a
breathtaking view of the whole church, while the
other leads straight to the altar and a place of
prayer.

People can spend all their lives on the circular
path, travelling the world, marvelling at all they
see, but those who truly appreciate the wonders of
the world take the straight path – and say thanks
to the Architect.

"Yours, O Lord, is the greatness and the power
and the glory and the majesty and the splendour,
for everything in heaven and earth is yours."
                    (Chronicles 1 29:11)

Monday — *August 8*

"THE most noteworthy thing about gardeners," wrote novelist Vita Sackville-West, "is that they are always optimistic, always enterprising and never satisfied. They always look forward to doing better than they have ever done before."

Fine words to take with you as you step out with your trowel! And for those who don't spend much time with the flowers and the vegetable patch — well, why not take these words with you as you venture out, and look on your life as the biggest garden of all?

Tuesday — *August 9*

LIFE has its peaks and troughs but through all the ups and downs some things are constant and dependable. As the historian George T. Hewitt wrote during the Second World War:

"The best things in life are never rationed. Friendship, loyalty and love do not require coupons."

It was true back then, and it has been ever since!

Wednesday — *August 10*

I'M sure we all want to be able to reach out to others, to help those who might be less fortunate. But it's easier said than done, isn't it?

When it comes down to the physical reality of reaching out to a stranger we often stumble, uncertain how to proceed. Agnes Bojaxhiu, better known as Mother Teresa, gave us all this advice:

"Love others the way that God has loved you —

with tenderness."

FAITHFUL FOLLOWERS

Thursday — *August 11*

OUR friend John had been putting off mowing the lawn for a while. Laziness? Well, maybe a little, but mostly it was because the grass had the most beautiful scattering of daisies.

As Therese of Lisieux said: "The splendour of the rose and the whiteness of the lily do not rob the little violet of its scent, nor the daisy of its simple charm. If every tiny flower wanted to be a rose, Spring would lose its loveliness."

It's a thought that's as valid for us as it is for flowers. If only we could learn to be more content in ourselves. And so for a while John was content to let the grass grow just a little bit higher as he sat enjoying the "simple charm" of his daisies . . .

Friday — *August 12*

THE theologian Hans Kung was once interviewed on radio about his beliefs. The panel was prepared to hear a deeply intellectual commentary.

The interviewer asked him in reverential tones what lay at the heart of his faith, and the great man took his audience completely by surprise by leaning close to the microphone and singing softly, "Jesus loves me."

Saturday — *August 13*

I THINK that generosity of spirit is a wonderful quality, a jewel in the crown of life. Something, surely, for all of us to cultivate. Lord Lytton put it this way:

"A good heart is better than all the heads in the world."

Sunday — **August 14**

D ARREN and Laura sold their home not long ago and intend to travel to Brazil. They would like to live there permanently with their four children, working as missionaries and helping the less fortunate.

It's a bold move to sell everything and leave all the familiarity and comforts of home behind. This young couple believe they have been called to this adventure. As they say, "There's a steep mountain before us, but the Lord will climb it with us."

It's been said that faith is not the absence of doubt, but the presence of trust: "He said to them, 'Go into all the world and preach the good news to all creation'." (Mark 16:15)

Monday — **August 15**

F I could open up my arms
And spread them really wide,
Why, even then I'd never get
The things I love inside.
For how can human arms embrace
A rainbow in the sky,
A daisy-studded meadow,
Or a billowed cloud on high?
No grasp could hold the starlight
Or a landscape full of snow,
No clasp could hold a Summer's day,
Not yet a sunset's glow.
But still I open wide my arms
To offer God my praise
For giving us this lovely world
To cherish all our days.

Margaret Ingall.

Tuesday — *August 16*

I'M sure we all know better than to judge a book by its cover — but that doesn't mean examples of why it's wrong can't still make us wince or smile.

Take the story about country singer Lonzo Green. His nephew Jimmy made a new friend, but this friend lived on the rough, poor side of town and Jimmy's parents didn't allow him to visit.

Jimmy's friend had a guitar but it needed tuning, so they took it to Uncle Lonzo. Despite the stares and abuse the boy attracted Lonzo invited him in, tuned the guitar and chatted about music for a while.

Lonzo and Jimmy had the right idea and the neighbours were wrong to judge. The boy from the wrong side of town was called Elvis — Elvis Presley.

Wednesday — *August 17*

LITTLE things can make a big difference, without doubt. Maggie had spent the whole afternoon working on her front garden.

"It's not very big," she told the Lady of the House, "and because I live near town, it gets its fair share of traffic fumes and litter. Trying to keep the plants and shrubs looking good can be difficult, and I'd just decided it was hardly worth the effort, when a young man strolling by paused and called out, 'That's lovely!' and walked on.

"Just two words," Maggie said, "but they made me realise that my garden was being noticed, and that certainly made a difference to how I felt about looking after it."

Isn't it amazing what a little appreciation can do? So let's all make sure we hand it out more often!

Thursday — *August 18*

HAVE you ever heard the story of a small bird that lived in a forest? One hot Summer's day, a terrible fire started and the flames devoured many trees and animals. Other birds flew away to safety, but the small bird couldn't bear to let her beloved home burn.

Day and night, she flew back and forth to the river, filling her beak with water to drop on the inferno. The small bird's courage and perseverance moved the angels to shed an abundance of tears and a great downpour of rain fell upon the forest, extinguishing the flames.

From this tale we learn that even the smallest actions of the brave and determined can change the world.

Friday — *August 19*

FRIENDSHIP is a union of spirits, a marriage of hearts. William Penn.

Saturday — *August 20*

LOOKING around the Museum of Scotland in Edinburgh our friend Charles' eye was drawn to a little block of coal. This was, unusually, a lump of coal carved into the shape of a Bible, crafted by a Lithuanian miner fleeing Russian persecution in the 1930s.

Proof, if it were needed, that no matter how deep in the dark we are, no matter how far from home we may be, no matter how unimportant and forgotten we might feel, we can carry God with us in a willing heart.

Sunday — **August 21**

EACH year a well-known publishing firm chooses a new word they think will be influential in the years ahead.

Do you recognise "groceteria" or "bovrilise"? They were unsuccessful attempts at describing "supermarkets" and "condensed". But how right they were in 1902 when they predicted the phrase "teddy bear" would soon catch on.

The compilers have been right — and wrong — with their choice of words, just like we can be when we speak without thinking, but it doesn't need to be a difficult choice. Jesus is the living embodiment of "The Word" and he's been getting it right for over two millennia.

"The Word is very near to you; it is in your mouth and in your heart so you may obey it."

(Deuteronomy 30:14)

Monday — **August 22**

TO those who study human behaviour it's all a bit of a puzzle, one they regularly come up with different theories to explain. I'm talking about altruism, that strange habit we have of doing things for others without thought for ourselves.

It seems to be the very opposite of a survival mechanism — until, that is, we look at ourselves as part of something bigger.

"I wonder if you realise a deep, great fact," Friedrich von Hugel wrote in the nineteenth century. "That all human souls are interconnected. That we can not only pray for each other but suffer for each other?"

Like one big family, perhaps . . .

Tuesday — **August 23**

WE have never been short of people telling us what can't be done. In 1899 the director of the patents office declared: "Everything that can be invented has been invented."

In 1895 Lord Kelvin, a well-known scientist, informed everyone, "Heavier than air flying machines are not possible."

So next time someone tells you that something is impossible, just listen to the only expert that really matters — your heart — and do it anyway!

Wednesday — **August 24**

IT'S a paradox that while we all love to have friends, sometimes the thought of taking steps to make new ones can be daunting.

Happily, some excellent advice comes from the lips of A. A. Milne's character Winnie the Pooh, who says: "You can't stay in your corner of the Forest waiting for others to come to you. You have to go to them sometimes."

Not such a Bear of Very Little Brain after all!

Thursday — **August 25**

THERE'S an old Welsh tale told of a man who quarrelled with his sweetheart. He still wanted to marry her but she refused to hear his proposal.

So the spurned suitor could only slip a love letter under her door — and he did this once a week for forty-two years! Aged seventy-four she accepted his proposal and the couple were married.

God sends us a message with each new dawn and waits, like a patient suitor, for us to hear him.

Friday — *August 26*

IN heavenly places I see my Father's face
where least expected —
In a child's eyes,
A newborn blade of grass,
A mother's loving touch.
In a humming bird hovering at my window,
A meadow soaked in sunlight,
Or a kind word.
Often, I find Him waiting for me
In heavenly places —
Those ordinary moments
Where I never thought to look.

Rachel Wallace–Oberle.

Saturday — *August 27*

THESE words, I believe, can help all of us, whatever challenges we are facing:

"Do not fear the winds of adversity. Remember the kite rises against the wind rather than with it."

Sunday — *August 28*

OUR old friend Mary, who finds great pleasure in the world of nature, said to me one day:

"You know, when I am troubled I look to the hills. Whether snow-capped or patterned with Summer clouds, their age-old, cool detachment from the hurly-burly of daily life calms the mind. They give a new perspective to concerns and worries."

As the twenty-first Psalm says:

I to the hill will lift mine eyes, from whence doth come mine aid.

Monday — **August 29**

WHEN we go about our daily business we often have no real idea what the others we meet might be going through, or just what a help a sunny disposition might be. And because we never know, we should always put our best attitude forward . . . just in case.

Emily Dickinson described it this way:
They might not need me; but they might.
I'll let my head be just in sight;
A smile as small as mine might be
Precisely their necessity.

Tuesday — **August 30**

CAN there be anything sweeter in the world than talking to an old friend and discovering they cherish the recollection of something you did but have long since forgotten?

This is summed up well in this Native American saying, "The memories we give may a lifetime live in the hearts of those we hold so close."

Wednesday — **August 31**

ONE of the most useful pieces of advice Sylvia was ever given was, "If you're wondering if it's right or wrong, ask yourself what would the world be like if everyone did it?"

But the nineteenth-century Bishop and author Phillips Brooks had a much more positive way of comparing yourself with everyone else. "Be such a person and live such a life," he wrote, "that if everyone were such as you, and every life such as yours, the earth would be God's paradise."

September

ISAK Dinesen, the author of "Out Of Africa", was actually Baroness Karen Blixen and in her writings is to be found the closest thing I have perhaps ever found to a universal panacea.

"The cure for anything," she wrote, "is salt water. Tears, sweat, or the sea."

Tears? Well, we all feel better after a good cry. Sweat? Well, that would be the effort we put into making a bad situation better. And there's nothing like a stroll by the seaside to soothe the spirit – or raise it as the need may be.

NOTHING'S gained without an effort,
No battles won without a fight,
Never let your heart be heavy
Dawn will always follow night.

Never a road without a turn,
Seek and find a better way,
Look ahead, the path is smoother,
There will come a brighter day.

Never let the worries harm you,
Or the doubt and fear begin,
There will be a new tomorrow,
Keep the light of hope within!

Iris Hesselden.

Saturday — *September 3*

I'VE often admired Rhian for her positive attitude to life, so I wasn't surprised to learn that, at an age when most people are slowing down, she had decided to enter a marathon.

"The best advice I've been given about training," she told me, "is that when doing my practice runs, I should always try to go a little farther than I'm comfortable with."

Her words made me think, for so often we don't tend to push our boundaries, whether mental or physical. And although it's certainly easier to stay within the safe and comfortable limits of our routines, it doesn't actually take us very far.

So let's take inspiration from Rhian, and even if we have no plans to don running shoes, we can still try to challenge ourselves to go that extra mile!

Sunday — *September 4*

EACH morning our old friend Mary reads from a devotional book that belonged to her grand-mother. Its strongest message is that we should try repeating often to ourselves these three words: *All is well.*

This well-thumbed book teaches us that even when life seems particularly challenging, we can look to a higher authority and trust that Someone will carry us through.

"Many times I've said to myself that all is well," Mary told me. "Even when it didn't appear so, and my faith has been increased and my mood lifted."

"You are my hiding place; you will protect me from trouble and surround me with songs of deliverance." (Psalms 32:7)

Monday — **September 5**

THE shock-haired image of Albert Einstein has become a standard sight on students' walls the world over. The great physicist is rightly admired and looked up to. Who did Einstein have on his wall — so to speak — to inspire him?

The answer is Scottish scientist James Clerk Maxwell. And, in turn, he looked up to somebody.

"What is done by what is called myself," he wrote, "is, I feel, done by something greater than myself in me."

It's always good to have someone to look up to. Just make sure you look up high enough.

Tuesday — **September 6**

THESE are words supposedly passed on by an elderly lady in America's Deep South to a young man complaining about life's hardships.

"Son," she said, "if the mountains were smooth you'd never be able to climb them."

What a thought!

Wednesday — **September 7**

WHEN setting out on a long walk you should always be prepared. You might take strong boots if the terrain is rough or sunscreen on a hot day. But no matter what the walk or what the conditions may be like, hymn writer Henry Van Dyke reminds us of the one essential travelling aid we should always try to have:

Our road will be smooth and untroubled
No matter what care life may send;
If we travel the pathway together,
And walk side by side with a friend.

Thursday — *September 8*

IN his classic work, "The Imitation Of Christ", Thomas à Kempis wrote: "The glory of a good man is the testimony of a good conscience.

"Therefore, keep your conscience good and you will always enjoy happiness, for a good conscience can bear a great deal and can bring joy even in the midst of adversity . . . Sweet shall be your rest if your heart does not reproach you."

Friday — *September 9*

IF you like to write a journal,
Then your story it will chart,
If you love recalling people,
Keeping photos can be smart,
But oh, please do remember,
Though such records play their part,
Memories keep freshest when
They're tucked inside your heart.
Margaret Ingall.

Saturday — *September 10*

BEN is in his sixties and still a student. He works full-time and attends university, taking courses in the evenings.

Over the years, his degrees have steadily accumulated, yet he intends to continue learning and improving his mind for as long as he can. Last year he accepted the offer of a twelve-month placement two hundred miles away.

Ben likes to quote this thought provoking saying when asked why he's not interested in retirement: "Learning is a treasure that accompanies its owner everywhere."

Sunday — *September 11*

I JUST *don't have time!* It's a catchphrase which seems to encapsulate the pace of life in the twenty-first century. So often we fall into the trap of continually rushing from place to place, trying to cram in as many things as possible, and all in the hope that it will bring us a sense of fulfilment.

But to me, there is one thing which is absolutely essential to true fulfilment, and that is time itself. Time to sit and stare, to think about the important things of life and to enjoy being alive and part of such an amazing world.

If in doubt, we need only to look to the Bible to inspire us: "And God blessed the seventh day, and sanctified it: because that in it he had rested from all his work which God created and made."

(Genesis 2:3)

Monday — *September 12*

"**W**OULD you be an angel and take my books back to the library on your way?" the Lady of the House asked as I prepared to go out one day.

It's such a common expression, isn't it? — *Be an angel.* And yet I suspect none of us believe that we really could be an angel, for that involves far more than we mortals could ever be capable of.

However, I rather like the words of writer Joan Wester Anderson, who said: "We can all be angels to one another. We can choose to obey the still small stirring within, the little whisper that says, 'Go. Ask. Reach out. Be an answer to someone's plea. You have a part to play. Have faith'."

Perhaps being an angel isn't completely impossible. After all, we've nothing to lose by trying!

Tuesday — *September 13*

OUR friend Hamish was puzzled for a moment when a friend from the Scottish Highlands told him, "Whit wouldna mak' a pot would mak' a pot lid."

Then the penny dropped. It used to take a big lump of iron to form into a pot that would be sturdy enough to sit on a fire and hold porridge or soup or stew. A smaller piece of metal on top of the pot would keep the heat in. A very important job!

In other words we all have our strengths and talents. One isn't better than the other, we're just different.

Wednesday — *September 14*

EVER wondered why tennis players refer to zero points as "Love"? One theory says at that point in the game you aren't a contender for the prize, so you must be playing for the love of the game.

It's an idea that might be carried through into other aspects of life, such as our relationships with friends, family and neighbours. How different all our lives would be if our actions were decided, not by points or profit, but by the love of the game.

Now, that would be a prize worth playing for!

Thursday — *September 15*

HENRY Blinn, an elder of the Shaker church, wanted us to know we can each make the world a brighter place, when he wrote: "Begin today. No matter how feeble the light, let it shine as best it may. The world may just need that quality of light which you have."

Friday — *September 16*

THE Babemba tribe in South Africa have a novel way of dealing with wrongdoers. They make the person concerned stand alone in the middle of the village, all work ceases and all the villagers gather in a circle around the person who has stepped out of line.

Then they take turns at recalling every good thing he or she has ever done — sometimes this can take a long time. Then they are welcomed back into their family community.

If we shun a person for one wrong deed, then we risk missing out on every good thing they might do in the future. So let's keep the idea of a day of appreciation and forgiveness like the Babemba in mind.

Saturday — *September 17*

I WONDER how many of us who have donated blood, or have had a blood transfusion, have heard of Dr Charles Drew? He was an African American physician and surgeon born in 1904.

Dr Drew was a clever medical researcher, and he made the important discovery of how to efficiently store large quantities of blood plasma in blood banks for future use. He also established the American Red Cross Blood Bank.

Latterly, Charles Drew held the post of Professor of Surgery at Howard University in Washington but was only forty-six years old when he died. He achieved much for the benefit of mankind, and every day many lives throughout the world continue to be saved as the direct result of his pioneering research.

Sunday — *September 18*

MARY Chapin Carpenter is a singer-songwriter who takes it as a compliment when others ask to cover her work.

"It's a marvellous feeling when someone says, 'I want to do this song of yours.' It means they've connected to it and that's what I'm after," she says.

It's the same kind of feeling when you live a life in the footsteps of the Lord, when your example encourages others to say, "I want to share this faith of yours." It means they have connected:

" 'Bring them here to me,' he said."

(Matthew 14:18)

Monday — *September 19*

WE all like to receive presents. Some will have caused great excitement, some will have touched the heart and their importance will have had nothing to do with their size.

This very point was emphasised by Florence Nightingale, when she said, "Life is the most splendid gift — and there is nothing small about it!"

Tuesday — *September 20*

WHO hasn't stopped and watched in awe as flocks of birds fly overhead, heading south in their V-shaped formations at this time of year?

It's always an impressive sight and, somehow, just a little sad. For with the birds go their songs.

But don't despair — they will be back! As Mary Webb, a romantic novelist of the early twentieth century, pointed out, "Nature's music is never over. Her silences are pauses, not conclusions."

Wednesday — **September 21**

I WONDER if you know the story of Antoni Gaudi, who became known as "God's architect". It is one of courage, patience and faith in adversity.

Antoni was born in Catalonia in 1852 and trained as an architect in Barcelona. Inspired by Catalan, Christian and Moorish culture, he developed his own individual style using patterned brick, stone, bright ceramic tiles and distinctive metal work.

From 1882 Gaudi began to devote almost all his time to the design and building of his monumental church in Barcelona dedicated to the Holy Family, La Sagrada Familia.

His last years were dogged by personal sorrows and lack of money to continue the building of La Sagrada Familia, which he saw as "the last great sanctuary of Christendom", but "God's architect" did not give up. He held fast, and struggled on with his great endeavour to create "a place of fraternity for all". He died in June 1926, after being knocked down by a tram and was buried in his unfinished masterpiece.

Today many thousands visit La Sagrada Familia where work continues, funded from sources which share its creator's vision. It is hoped that the great church will be completed to mark the one hundredth anniversary of Gaudi's death.

Thursday — **September 22**

MOST of my ills I have cured,
And the worst I have always survived.
But the very worst ones I've endured —
Were those that never arrived.

GLORIOUS GAUDI

Friday — *September 23*

HERE are three thought-provoking quotes to share today about that priceless gift, laughter:

"The world is as a looking-glass and gives back to every man the reflection of his own face. Frown at it and it in turn will look sourly upon you; laugh at it and with it, and it is a jolly, kind companion."

William Makepeace Thackeray.

"The human race has one really effective weapon, and that is laughter."   Mark Twain.

"Laughter is a holy thing. It is as sacred as music and silence and solemnity, maybe more sacred. Laughter is like a prayer, like a bridge over which creatures tiptoe to meet each other. Laughter is like mercy, it heals. When you can laugh at yourself, you are free."   Ted Loda.

Saturday — *September 24*

AUTUMN brings the first frosts of Winter, still, misty mornings, shorter days and lengthening afternoon shadows. We turn our clocks back, and the highest hills are soon topped with their first white quilting of snow.

Thomas Tusser wrote in his "Five Hundreth Pointes of Good Husbandry" in the sixteenth century: "September blow soft till fruit be in loft". Is there anything more evocative of Autumn than the sharp, aromatic scent of apples, and the sweet smell of pears stored away safely for Winter?

Throughout the ages seedtime and harvest have been immeasurably important to mankind, and we give thanks when the harvest is safely gathered in. There is something very reassuring in the turning of the seasons.

THE FRIENDSHIP BOOK

Sunday — *September 25*

*L*ORD, I pray that you would teach me to mother
  my children in the way you father me.
Fill me with your wisdom so that I can guide
    their paths.
Fill me with your grace and compassion so I can
    love them unconditionally.
Fill me with your strength so that I will make the
    right choices for them and myself.
Fill me with your joy so that I will pour into my
    home a love that covers, protects,
    encourages, nurtures and forgives.
Fill me with your peace so that I will always
    remember these little ones are yours.
Thank you for choosing me to guide and
    cherish them.
  — Amen.

Rachel Wallace-Oberle.

Monday — *September 26*

I'M coming to the conclusion that there are many
people in this world who are more than willing to
tell us how to run our lives yet not so keen to put
those guidelines into practice themselves," Greg
said one day after reading a bundle of newspapers.

I smiled, for his words brought to mind some
lines written by Edgar Guest:

I'd rather see a sermon, than hear one any day
I'd rather one should walk with me than merely
    tell the way . . .

"It's a reminder that we should aim to be the sort
of person who gets chosen as a walking companion, rather than the one who merely likes to give
out directions!"

Tuesday — *September 27*

CHRISTINE, who had been trying to arrange a concert of praise involving several different faiths, was sounding several opinions on what form it should take.

"All the responses were well intentioned," she said. "But they contradicted each other. Some felt it should be entirely serious, some wanted humour, some wanted drama, some said it should be nothing but classical recitals . . ."

Happily, the Lady of the House was able to come up with a quotation from Dean William Inge, which made us smile: "We should think of the church as an orchestra in which the different churches play on different instruments while a Divine Conductor calls the tune."

I like to believe that Someone will be able to unite all our efforts into sweet music!

Wednesday — *September 28*

"WHEN I first retired," our friend John said, "I wanted to use some of my extra spare time to help those in need.

"Fortunately, our village has several organisations open to volunteers, and I soon found myself helping out in all sorts of practical ways that I'd never thought of, such as giving lifts, D.I.Y. assistance, and even doing some gardening. Not only do I feel a useful member of the community, but I've also made many new friends."

It was Antoine de Saint-Exupery who said, "In giving, you are throwing a bridge across the chasm of your solitude." Wise words, ones which John would entirely agree with.

Thursday — **September 29**

"YOU must be kidding!" Our young friend Daniel had just been reading an e-mail joke, but it wasn't this that had prompted this reaction. It was the address of the original sender — *Friendsville*!

Surely there was no such place? Well, a quick online search identified a town called Friendsville in several communities in the United States alone.

Who wouldn't want to move to a place with such a lovely name, I thought. But why move? Why not smile and say hello to the people who live around us?

Help and be open to help, extend a hand, show an interest, and we can make our own Friendsville just where we are.

Friday — **September 30**

WHEN John Todd was six years old his parents died. A kind aunt welcomed the distraught boy into her home. She became like a mother to him and Todd grew up to become a clergyman.

When he heard that his aunt was dying, he wrote to her, saying: "Years ago I left a house of death not knowing where I was going, whether anyone cared, or if that was the end of me. The journey was long but your servant encouraged me.

"I was welcomed by your warm embrace to a new home. I felt safe. You did all this for me, now it's your turn to go. I'm writing to let you know someone will be waiting for you. Your room's ready, the light's on, the door's open and they're expecting you.

"I know this because once, long ago, I saw God standing in your doorway."

October

ONE day at a village market our friend John stopped at a stall to look at the handicrafts on offer. The seller had painted some attractive signs that featured various quotes and sayings — John's favourite was this one:

Autumn is the year's last loveliest smile.

What a wonderful way to describe the richness of Autumn, don't you think?

THERE are few images more familiar to us than someone carrying an umbrella, but it wasn't always so. Two hundred years ago Jonas Hanway introduced the umbrella to London after travelling in the Far East.

People ridiculed him for it and cab drivers, who made their living from people caught in showers, tried to run him down. Undeterred, he persevered and now the trusty brolly is an everyday item.

Living a life of faith can be difficult at times, too, but like Jonas Hanway, we need to show people how it works, and demonstrate the ways in which it enriches our lives.

"So the word of God spread. The number of disciples in Jerusalem increased rapidly and a large number of priests became obedient to the faith"

(Acts 6:7)

Monday — **October 3**

I EXPECT to pass through this world but once — therefore, if there be any kindness I can show or any good thing I can do to any fellow human being, let me do it today; let me not defer or neglect it, for I shall not pass this way again.

William Penn.

Tuesday — **October 4**

OVER the years, I've discovered that if there's one thing that all great men and women have in common, it's the ability to keep faith with their ideas, no matter how much discouragement they meet on their way.

Eleanor Roosevelt put it rather more poetically: "The future belongs to those who believe in the beauty of their dreams."

Wednesday — **October 5**

LEGEND records that in Pictish times St Kessock visited the Holy Land. He brought back some dried fish from the Sea of Galilee, blessed them, threw them into what is now the Moray Firth in Scotland and told them to be fruitful and multiply.

When God granted them life again, they increased so abundantly that the small, sweet fish became famous nationwide as Kessock herring. Thereupon St Kessock taught local people how to preserve them as kippers.

His name is immortalised in the villages of South and North Kessock and since 1982 by the Kessock Bridge that links Inverness to the Black Isle.

Thursday — *October 6*

GEORGE has had more than one career during his working life and not through choice. Redundancies have left him unemployed on several occasions but each time, he retrained and made his way back up the career ladder. It has all led to a varied and interesting life.

George could have accepted defeat at any time, but instead he became a living example of the words of Canadian-born physician Oswald Avery:

"Whenever you fall, pick something up."

Friday — *October 7*

*I LOOKED upon my garden, and I couldn't help
  but frown
To see the sad Autumnal leaves so swiftly
  whirling down.
I thought of all the sweeping up, and grumbled
  loud and long,
And then I paused a moment, for I realised
  I was wrong.
For should the trees not shed their leaves that
  surely would deny
The sight of graceful Winter boughs beneath a
  frosty sky.
And, oh, I'd miss the Springtime buds in every
  woodland glade,
And in the heat of Summer, how I'd miss their
  dappled shade.
So let the leaves keep drifting down, my grumbles
  you won't hear,
For leaves are things of beauty, yes — whatever
  time of year.*

Margaret Ingall.

Saturday — *October 8*

MICHAEL was laughing as he arrived at his parents' house. "Well, I've often heard the expression that we should 'try walking a mile in another man's shoes', but I never thought I'd end up doing it!"

He went on to explain that he and a friend had been out for a walk that day, and after pausing for lunch at his sister's house each had unwittingly put on the other's boots to finish the journey.

"No wonder we ended up with sore feet," he grinned. "They sort of fitted but didn't really!"

We all enjoyed Michael's tale, yet it did make me think about the real truth of the saying he'd quoted. Fortunately, we don't usually have to demonstrate it so literally but next time we feel impatient with someone, it might be worth making that effort of imagination, for only then can we begin to understand someone else's difficulties — and perhaps appreciate our own good fortune.

Sunday — *October 9*

ROY Disney was seen as the inheritor of his Uncle Walt's vision. As head of the Disney organisation he had to make important decisions.

Asked how he dealt with these moments he said, "When your values are clear to you, making decisions becomes easier." Find your values and you'll find a yardstick for every situation.

"The Lord will guide you always; he will satisfy your needs in a sun-scorched land and will strengthen your frame. You will be like a well-watered garden, like a spring whose waters never fail." (Isaiah 58:11)

Monday — *October 10*

OPINIONS as to what's important and what's not seem to change with each succeeding generation, but some essential values stay the same, come what may. It's summed up nicely in these lines which the Lady of the House read in a favourite magazine:

Methods are many
Principles are few
Methods change often
Principles never do.

Tuesday — *October 11*

"HOW should I handle this?" we might ask. It could be a dispute between friends, an unexpected request or a chance to help someone.

Whatever the dilemma we can take help and guidance from these words by John Wesley:

Lord, who hast taught to us on earth
This lesson from above,
That all our works are nothing worth,
Unless they spring from love.

Wednesday — *October 12*

ARE you facing a challenge that you would rather not? It happens to all of us at times, so take heart from these observations:

"An inconvenience is only an adventure wrongly considered; an adventure is only an inconvenience rightly considered."   G. K. Chesterton.

"Great things are done when men and mountains meet."   William Blake.

Now, go and conquer those crags!

Thursday — *October 13*

"**I**'M very fond of Shona," Sally said, "but if only she wasn't always late for everything."

"Jeff is so generous about offering lifts," Grant observed, "but he has no sense of direction."

I suspect it would take a saint entirely to ignore other people's shortcomings, but I'm all for remembering these words from Lawrence G. Lovasik: "If, when you charged a person with his faults, you credited him with his virtues, too, you would probably like everybody."

Friday — *October 14*

I SMILED when I read actor Peter O'Toole's idea of a perfect epitaph. A leather jacket he'd had dry-cleaned was returned with a label saying, *It distresses me to return work that is not perfect.*

Let's face it, we will all be returned to our Maker in less than perfect condition but it will do no harm to spend the time we have getting rid of as many blemishes as we can.

Saturday — *October 15*

EXTRAORDINARY, isn't it, how as Autumn advances, nature puts on her most colourful show of the year? Gold, red and yellow are vivid colours just as lovely as the greens of Spring and Summer.

This beauty reminds me of the faces I see when I visit a local club for retired folk. There I see deep serenity, a glow that has come with the passage of years and a wealth of experience. In their Autumn they, too, have a deeper, stronger beauty.

Sunday — *October 16*

VISITORS to Westminster Abbey in London are often lost in amazement when they see the grandeur of the building. But before they get to stand between the magnificent pillars and gaze up at the high, vaulted ceilings, visitors pass through two sets of doors, an area called the narthex. In olden days travellers would remove wet robes and muddy boots there before entering the cathedral.

The narthex is like this life, a passageway from one world to another. It serves an important purpose and we can shelter there for a while — but the real glory waits beyond.

"For Christ did not enter a man-made sanctuary that was only a copy of the true one; he entered heaven itself, now to appear for us in God's presence." (Hebrews 9:24)

Monday — *October 17*

A WARM, comfortable home is a blessing indeed, but we shouldn't let a comfortable chair and thick walls cut us off from the greater blessings of the outside world.

One hundred and thirty years ago author Richard Jeffries offered advice for those "modern days" that holds good in the twenty-first century. In "The Amateur Poacher," he advised:

Let us get out of these indoor narrow
*   modern days,*
whose twelve hours somehow have
*   become shortened,*
into the sunlight and pure wind …
A something the ancients called divine
*   can be felt and found there still.*

Tuesday — **October 18**

HAVE you ever been to a rock concert? Or listened while an orchestra tackled one of their more dramatic scores?

We might jokingly say the noise would disturb the angels up above.

Henry Ward Beecher had his own opinion on which sounds travel farthest. "Of all earthly music," he wrote, "that which reaches farthest into Heaven is the beating of a truly loving heart."

Wednesday — **October 19**

" **I** PROMISE", "Cross my heart", "As God is my witness". Some folk go to great lengths to be believed — others don't have to say anything extra.

There's an old Turkish proverb that says, "A true word needs no oath", so let's try to live our lives in such a way that we don't need to make extravagant promises.

Thursday — **October 20**

NOT long after getting married Rudyard Kipling and his wife, Carrie, built themselves a home. They'd been there a year before they met the woman who lived on the hillside facing their own.

"Be ye the new lights across the valley yonder?" she asked. "You don't know what a comfort they've been to me this Winter."

As long as the Kiplings lived at "Naulakha" after this encounter they made sure the curtains on that side of the house remained undrawn. You never know who the light of your thoughtfulness reaches, so shine it brightly.

Friday — **October 21**

THE Lady of the House and I went to visit our friend Ted in hospital.

When we arrived he was sitting up in bed reading his Bible and I could not help noticing that it was very much the worse for wear. In fact, with its detached cover and crumpled and creased pages it looked in a sorry state.

"That Bible of yours has seen rather better days, Ted," I commented.

"Don't let that worry you," he replied. "Bibles that are falling apart are usually owned by people who aren't."

Now that's a statement I couldn't argue with.

Saturday — **October 22**

MY optimism disappeared
  For just a little while,
The world had lost its wonder
  The sun forgot to smile.
I felt a disappointment
  With people, places, things,
And I forgot the cheerfulness
  A bright new morning brings.

I looked at those around me
  Who bore a heavy load,
And knew that I was fortunate
  To walk a smoother road.
And I have faith and hope and love
  All these I never doubt,
My optimism has returned
  And now the sun's come out!
                    Iris Hesselden.

Sunday — *October 23*

ST THERESA is known as the Saint of the Little Ways, meaning she believed in doing the little things in life well and with infinite love. She is also the patron saint of flower growers and florists and is often represented by roses. A reader sent me St Theresa's Prayer and I'd like to share it with you:

May today there be peace within. May you trust God that you are exactly where you are meant to be. May you not forget the infinite possibilities that are born of faith.

May you use those gifts that you have received, and pass on the love that has been given to you. May you be content knowing you are a child of God. Let this presence settle into your bones, and allow your soul the freedom to sing, dance, praise and love.

It is there for each and every one of us. Amen.

Monday — *October 24*

I ADMIRE those who teach, and that's not, of course, confined to working in schools, for instructors come in all guises, and many of them would not even see themselves as teachers.

Nevertheless, that's what they do — whether it's the helpful neighbour who inspires others to play a part in community life, the experienced employee who helps newcomers to develop their abilities, or the parents who lovingly encourage their children to reach their full potential.

As Benjamin Disraeli said: "The greatest good you can do for another is not just share your riches, but reveal to them their own."

And that's a gift that will last a lifetime.

THE BEST OF FRIENDS

Tuesday — **October 25**

WHEN we think of philanthropists we might think of Tom Farmer, the Scottish millionaire who resolved to give all his money to good causes, Warren Buffett who made the world's biggest charitable donation, or perhaps Andrew Carnegie who funded public libraries all around the world.

You might not think there was much the ordinary person could do that would be as meaningful. But the word "philanthropy" comes from two Greek words, "philos" meaning "love" and "anthropos" meaning "man".

To do good in this world you don't have to be worth millions, you just have to be a loving man or a loving woman. Money can do a certain amount of good but it can never buy real philanthropy.

Wednesday — **October 26**

OUR old friend Mary's mother cherished this poem by Elizabeth Cheney in her collection of wise sayings. Since Mary's childhood it has, in turn, touched and inspired her and I hope it will do the same for you:

OVERHEARD IN AN ORCHARD

Said the Robin to the Sparrow,
"I would really like to know
why these anxious human beings
rush about and worry so."

Said the Sparrow to the Robin,
"Friend, I think that it must be
that they have no Heavenly Father
such as cares for you and me."

Thursday — **October 27**

ARE you familiar with the old saying that a trouble shared is a trouble halved? Janice certainly found it to be true when she met with a series of misfortunes, and her friend Jill helped her through.

That's why I smiled to see Janice carrying a large cake tin and walking in the direction of Jill's house.

"She's been so kind to me, that when I was baking, I made an extra batch of shortbread just for her," she explained. "After all, we shouldn't just share the bad things in life!"

Sigmund Freud once said, "When we share — that is poetry in the prose of life."

Friday — **October 28**

A TRUE friend is someone who thinks that you are a good egg even when he knows that you are slightly cracked!   Bernard Meltzer.

Saturday — **October 29**

THE harvest is gathered in, the branches are nearly bare. Are you feeling a bit dejected at the end of Summer? Don't forget — nature is already planning a revival.

The wild flower seeds that fell to the ground will bloom again next year. The buds forming on bushes and trees are waiting for the kiss of the sun to open them. Bulbs are slumbering in your garden till they awaken in the Spring.

The Summer whose glories we enjoyed so much has not gone forever. It has made preparations for a wonderful repeat performance.

Sunday — *October 30*

DO you sometimes take the world for granted? It can be easy to do so but then something stops us in our tracks. Perhaps we are ill or have an accident, yet unexpectedly we discover how rich we are in kind friends. Or perhaps, more happily, we might take a holiday and suddenly see anew the beauty of the world around us.

Let's make the effort to ensure these thank-you moments occur more often. There is so much to be grateful for, if we just take time to stop and reflect.

"Bless the Lord, O my soul, and forget not all his benefits."   (Psalms 103:2)

Monday — *October 31*

LAST night I saw a shooting star
  Its green tail through the sky;
I stood and watched until it passed
  Grew pale, began to die.

I thought of all the things I wished
  For me and me alone;
What I could do with my great wealth
  Far off and in my home.

Then I felt ashamed and thought
  Of those who had no wealth,
Who suffered poverty and shame and need
  Who never had good health.

I looked again and wished instead
  That I might share what God
In all His goodness blessed me with
  And spread His love abroad.

                                              Kenneth Steven.

November

Tuesday — **November 1**

ONE of the songs Tracey has always liked is "With A Little Help From My Friends", and a news item set her humming it once again.

Back in 1999 a group of friends gathered together in San Francisco. Commiserating with each other over the difficulties of creative writing, they made a pact that they would each try to pen a novel, meeting every night for a month to support each other's endeavours.

To their surprise, this approach worked so successfully that there is now an annual Novel Writing Month, starting on 1st November in which thousands of people take part, many of them even finishing on 30th, the deadline.

Now, it's not everyone's ambition to write a book, but I think this experiment speaks volumes for the power of friendship and moral support. "With a little help from my friends" almost anything can be achieved.

Wednesday — **November 2**

I'M sure most of us know what kind of lining every cloud is supposed to have – according to the old saying, that is. But I liked this take on the matter, seen in a magazine from the early 1900s:

"Don't worry if the cloud overhead looks dark. It's just the shadow cast by the silver lining!"

Thursday — **November 3**

AUTHOR A. J. Cronin provided the perfect justification for showing the sunnier side of our personality when he wrote: "On the smiles, the thanks we give, our little gestures of appreciation, our neighbours build up their philosophy of life."

Friday — **November 4**

A WORLD without suffering sounds so desirable, doesn't it? After all, what purpose could our trials and tribulations serve, we might ask?

A Franciscan monk, Father Andrew, offers his insight. "If suffering went out of life," he wrote, "courage, tenderness, pity, faith and love in its divinity would go out of life, too."

If those life-affirming qualities are the consequences, I will happily put up with a setback or two!

Saturday — **November 5**

FEW who heard it can ever forget the speech given by Barack Obama in Chicago on 5th November, 2008. It was just after he had won the election and been declared President Elect of the United States.

He spoke of his hopes and aspirations for the nation, his resolve to work for the betterment of all. But it was not all fine words and rhetoric. To his young daughters Sasha and Malia he said, "You have earned the new puppy that's coming with us to the White House."

It was a homely touch that endeared him to the crowd and moved the hearts of millions.

Sunday — **November 6**

AS a child Anna was afraid of the dark. She had trouble sleeping and imagined all sorts of frightening things as she lay tossing and turning.

One day, Anna's aunt prayed along with her that guardian angels would be present around her bed every night. She printed out this verse from her computer and put it in a frame: "I will lie down and sleep in peace, for you alone, O Lord, make me dwell in safety." (Psalms 4:8)

When we put our trust completely in our heavenly Father we can face all things with strength and confidence. As Dorothy Bernard once said, "Courage is fear that has said its prayers."

Monday — **November 7**

HERE are some lines written in celebration of long Winter evenings, and the joy of having a home and hearth. They were written by William Ernest Henley in the nineteenth century. His daughter, Margaret, who died aged six, was J. M. Barrie's model for Wendy in "Peter Pan".

O Winter, ruler of the inverted year,
I crown thee king of intimate delights,
Fireside enjoyments, home born happiness,
And all the comforts that the lowly roof
Of undisturbed retirement, and the hours
Of long uninterrupted eve'nings know.

William and Robert Louis Stevenson became friends when both were unknown writers. Their long friendship had its ups and downs, but that did not prevent R.L.S. from making William a small allowance when he was having money troubles.

Such is the essence of friendship.

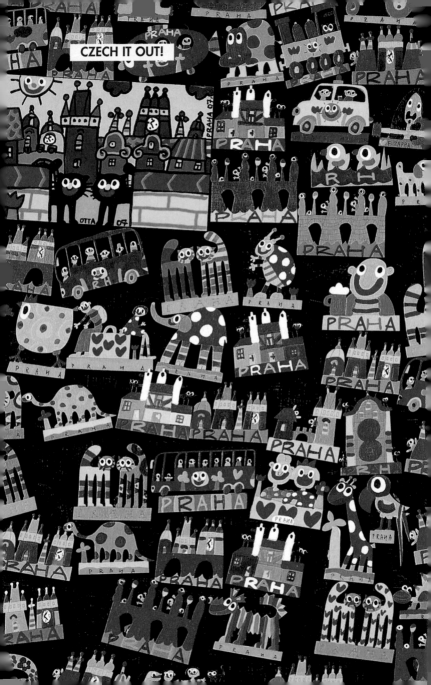

Tuesday — **November 8**

VINCENT Van Gogh had many fine attributes, not least of which was his renowned artistic ability. But he was prone to bouts of depression. These, however, didn't make him any less a genius.

As he said, "It is true that there is an ebb and flow but the sea remains the sea."

You might have good days and bad but, just like the sea, you'll always be you. And that's wonderful.

Wednesday — **November 9**

WHILE organising a Himalayan expedition, the Scottish mountaineer William Murray wrote: "Until one is committed there is hesitancy, the chance to draw back . . . (But) the moment one commits oneself then Providence moves, too, raising in one's favour all manner of unforeseen incidents, meetings and assistance which no man could have dreamt would come his way."

Take those first few steps and you'll be surprised what can be achieved.

Thursday — **November 10**

BY what standards do you judge a life? Is a person seen to be a success because they are famous or because they are wealthy?

The real answer is surely much simpler. Madeleine L'Engle summed it up this way:

"In the evening of life we shall be judged on love, and not one of us is going to come off very well, and were it not for my absolute faith in the loving forgiveness of my Lord, I would not call Him to come."

Friday — *November 11*

THE tactics had all been discussed and, as the under-elevens football team ran out to give their best in a local tournament, the coach shouted after them, "Remember, it's team work that makes the dream work!"

I'm sure that the young players will remember these words for there aren't many dreams worth having that only involve one person. Dreams are somehow bigger when we share them.

Our team might be family, friends, workmates or just you and your partner, but the dream will turn out so much better, and be so much sweeter, if you arrive there as a team.

Saturday — *November 12*

GOD has signed His signature
Across the midnight sky,
His hands have placed the stars in space
Beyond the naked eye.
On snowflakes, birds and butterflies
And waves upon the sea,
On seashells on the sandy shore
His fingerprints we see.

Mountain peaks and singing streams
The clouds, the earth, the land,
Each living thing all bears the stamp
Of His creative hand.
In colour, texture and design
On blossom, bud and tree,
He leaves His hallmark everywhere
For those with eyes to see.

Kathleen Gillum.

Sunday — **November 13**

JAZZ musician Duke Ellington learned about life in noisy clubs and on rough streets. His was an education in the School of Hard Knocks. Very little of his learning came from books, but one book helped him make sense of it all.

"On becoming more acquainted with the word of the Bible, I began to understand so much more of what I had been taught, and about what I had learned about life and the people in mine."

"To God belong wisdom and power, counsel and understanding are His."

(Job 12:13)

Monday — **November 14**

I WAS initially taken aback to read of a young man called Juan Mann who had taken to standing on the streets of Sydney holding a placard offering "Free Hugs". A surprisingly large number of people took him up on the offer, and even those who didn't enjoyed seeing him there.

"For every person who gets a hug, you will see five more walk past with a smile on their face," he said.

The authorities were less impressed, and for a while it seemed the Free Hugs Campaign might be banned. But within days a petition of more than ten thousand signatures had been presented to the City of Sydney Council asking for it to continue. Today this idea is as successful as ever, and seems set to spread to other places.

It's a wonderful reminder of the fact that even a small gesture can achieve an enormous amount of good.

Tuesday — **November 15**

THE eastern concept of Karma translates as "action". The belief is that the good or bad deeds you put into the universe will come back to you.

The Bible says, "As you sow, so must you reap," and Isaac Newton enshrined the principle in his Third Law of Motion: "For every action there is an equal and opposite re-action."

Then folk wisdom advises us that "What goes around comes around", so let's ensure that the actions we cause to "go around" are seen as welcome gifts when they "come around".

Wednesday — **November 16**

ALBERT Einstein's research lit the way for many scientists and thinkers to follow. But his own favourite concepts had nothing to do with relativity, black holes or the speed of light — they were things we could all appreciate.

"The ideas that lit my way," Einstein wrote, "have been kindness, beauty and truth." These qualities are every bit as important to the universe!

Thursday — **November 17**

DO you ever wonder what home life's like for the famous? Well, the fixtures and fittings might be different but if there are children involved I imagine the basics would be the same.

Children, especially babies, are great levellers. A point not missed by the anonymous sage who wrote: "Home is where the great are small — and the small are great!"

SANCTUARY

Friday — *November 18*

WHEN astronomers talk about planets capable of sustaining life, they often refer to "the Goldilocks Zone". What does that mean? Well, it's when the planet isn't too close to the sun, or too far away, just like in the children's tale where Baby Bear's soup was neither too hot, nor too cold.

Our lives can be seen the same way. We have problems and we have good times, but most of us never go to the extremes of either option. We tend, most of the time, to stay in that zone where things are neither too bad, nor too good, but are, as Goldilocks said with a sigh, "Just right!"

Saturday — *November 19*

I WAS struck by this line from a minister's sermon: "If we really believe we are the children of God, should we not call home more often?"

Sunday — *November 20*

MORRIS had taken his daughter to a sub-aqua lesson and he was sharing pearls of wisdom.

"No matter how interesting it is," he said, "never forget the way to safety. Always keep in your mind the best way to get straight to the top."

There are millions of fascinating distractions in this world and not all of them are safe. That's why, whatever we are doing, it helps to have practised the safest, quickest way to get straight to the top.

"I will spread out my hands in prayer to the Lord. The thunder will stop and there will be no more hail, so you may know that the earth is the Lord's."
(Exodus 9:29)

Monday — **November 21**

OUR old friend Mary told us about a recent wedding she'd attended.

"During the ceremony, something was said that has stayed with me," she told us. "The clergyman was talking about how Alan and Gillian should treat each other and suggested that, while doing the right thing was important, they should guard against being determined to always be right.

" 'What's important is not being right, but being kind,' he'd said."

It's true — so often we are determined to prove a point and show that we were right in some trivial matter or other. Surely the best relationships are those in which both parties can step back, stop insisting that they know best, and simply forget who supposedly won the argument.

Tuesday — **November 22**

IT'S different these days thanks to central heating and double glazing, but many of us will be able to recall Winter nights when noses and ears were icy while the rest of us felt as warm as toast under the blankets.

The following day we'd see what complicated lacy patterns the crisp frost had etched on the windows. Such memories are wonderful when viewed from a warm, modern perspective. And what made me think of them were these words by Bill Morgan Jr.:

Winter came down to our home one night
Quietly pirouetting in
On silver-toed slippers of snow,
And we, we were children once again.

Wednesday — *November 23*

OUR friend John was recalling his schooldays as he walked along beside the river one afternoon where he had often played with friends when young. It all seemed so different now, he mused.

Then he arrived at the tree where he and some friends had tethered a raft under sheltering branches. That day he caught sight of another raft, complete with a children's flag flying in the breeze.

The words of the poet Samuel Woodworth came to mind: "How dear to the heart are the scenes of my childhood, when fond recollection presents them to my view."

Thursday — *November 24*

WE see the sunlight dancing
And listen to the lark,
But others feel the walls close in,
Their world is sad and dark.
The perfume of the roses
The scent of new-mown hay,
Unknown to many troubled hearts
Who walk a shadowed way.

The glory of the Autumn
The Winter sunset glow,
Can never touch those housebound souls
Whose days all come and go.
So when your day has promise
A rainbow arch above,
Send healing thoughts to those in need,
And plant fresh seeds of love.

Iris Hesselden.

Friday — **November 25**

I'VE been reading about Nola Ochs, who at the age of ninety-five was possibly the oldest person in the world to be awarded a college degree. It's an inspiring account, as indeed are most stories about those who have overcome age, adversity, even convention to achieve what they most want from life.

However, I wonder how many of us reading such stories sit back and think to ourselves, "Of course, I, too, could have done that if only . . ." But it's the "if onlys" and the too-ready excuses as to why we shouldn't which so often hold us back from reaching our full potential.

Consider these words by Don Wilder: "Excuses are the nails to build a house of failure." Instead of building a house of failure, let's aim to erect a monument to success.

Saturday — **November 26**

THIS thought on beauty was sent to me from a reader in Malawi. "Have you ever noticed how we women like to hold a mirror to our face before we go out? We want to make sure we look our best for the world.

"Well, I was thinking how nice it would be if we could hold a mirror to our hearts every day before we leave our homes. We could check we had enough love inside to share with others, repair the wounds made by disagreements and make sure our hearts are smiling when we go out."

Now, wouldn't that be wonderful? True beauty, of course, comes from within, and the heart is the perfect place to start.

Sunday — **November 27**

DON'T you find the early morning often sets the tone for the rest of the day? If you rise late, you tend to spend a while catching up. After all, if your morning's a muddled whirl of activity, why would the rest of the day be any different?

There's a Buddhist expression, *Penpa Tang*, that might help. It means taking time in the morning to set the tone for the kind of day you'd like to have.

This might involve meditation, a few minutes silence to focus your mind or a leisurely walk. You might also take the advice of King David:

"In the morning, O Lord, you hear my voice; in the morning I lay my requests before you and wait in expectation." (Psalms 5:3)

Monday — **November 28**

EVERY competitor at the Olympics hopes to win a medal, but the founder of the modern game, Baron de Coubertin, had higher hopes than simply winning, which is why he set up the International Fair Play Trophy.

The first such award was presented to Italian bobsledder Eugenio Monti. His two-man team was in the lead and only one other had a chance of beating him. Then he heard that a bolt on his opponent's bobsled had sheared before their final run. Monti took the equivalent bolt from his own sled and gave it to the team who went on to beat him.

Baron de Coubertin knew that the judges on the ground would see who crosses the line first, but a judge with a much higher viewpoint is watching how we play the game.

Tuesday — *November 29*

I HAVE friends who could talk the hind legs off the proverbial donkey and others who could double as walking dictionaries, because they know so many words. But I have a soft spot for Ernest and think that everyone should have a friend just like him.

When we go for a stroll it's often in silence, just appreciating the world around us. But if I speak, he gives me his full attention. He often reminds me of that old Scottish rhyme:

*His thoughts were slow, his words were few
And never formed to glisten.
But he was a joy to all the clan,
For you should have heard him listen!*

Wednesday — *November 30*

THE SECRET NIGHT

*A T night the stars in silver frost
Adorn the Winter sky;
Across the earth no creature stirs,
The fields in slumber lie.*

*I feel this night that only me
In all the wide world round
Can see the moon that climbs so white
And shines without a sound.*

*I watch it shine its silver light
So bright no thing can hide;
So bright that I could go and walk
Through all the country wide.*

Kenneth Steven.

December

Thursday — **December 1**

HERE is a tapestry of thoughts for December. It is the month of the Christmas tree, the festive scarlet and green poinsettia, the Christmas rose with its creamy-white flowers and red-berried holly, described by John Evelyn, the seventeenth-century diarist, as "glittering with its armed and varnished leaves, blushing with their natural coral".

Above all, December's thirty-one midwinter days see the great festival of Christmas, with its joyful celebration of the birth of the Christ Child in Bethlehem, told in the age-old words of St Luke: "For unto you is born this day in the city of David a Saviour, which is Christ the Lord".

December ends with Hogmanay, as it is known in Scotland, the doorway to a New Year. The days between Christmas and New Year are surely a perfect time for quiet reflection, a time to be thankful for our blessings, and to hope for peace, friendship and love in the world.

Friday — **December 2**

A LEGEND among film stars, Clint Eastwood's tenacity is legendary. He once said, "I don't believe in pessimism. If something doesn't come up the way you want, forge ahead. If you think it's going to rain, it will."

Wise words to think about today.

DEEP AND CRISP

Saturday — **December 3**

SMILING, they say, makes us look younger and generally creates a positive and confident sense of well-being. The Lady of the House was reminded of this when she caught sight of these words in a magazine:

It takes sixty muscles to frown but only thirteen to smile. Why waste energy?

Whenever people meet, a smile is an ice-breaker and it can even brighten the most sombre gatherings; the shortest distance between two people, they say, is a smile.

"A smile costs nothing. It enriches those who receive, without impoverishing those who give," observed writer and lecturer Dale Carnegie.

So let's make our journey through life a happy and healthy one for ourselves and others by beginning each mile with an "s"!

Sunday — **December 4**

THE great Polar explorer Fridtjof Nansen was also a professor of oceanography. Charting the depths of the oceans he used the basic technique of tying a lead weight to a length of rope. Eventually, he ran out of rope and at these points on the charts he wrote, *Deeper than that.*

There is a profound contentment that comes from knowing God and it is impossible to measure. When trying to describe it to others we may wish to borrow Nansen's expression and simply say it is "deeper than that".

"And the peace of God, which transcends all understanding, will guard your hearts and your minds in Jesus Christ." (Philippians 4:7)

Monday — *December 5*

OUR friend Mabel often arranges spontaneous "little celebrations". Friends, neighbours and family are invited to her home for the afternoon and tea is served, relaxing music is played and the supply of home-made cakes never runs out. These are always warm, happy times filled with lots of laughter and good company.

When the Lady of the House asked if the effort to host these get-togethers was becoming too much, she replied, "Not at all. As a saying I once read puts it, 'The ornaments of a house are the friends who frequent it'."

Tuesday — *December 6*

AN American correspondent informed me that she likes to save the quotes on little slips of paper hidden in Chinese fortune cookies. Here are two of her favourites:

Don't stand by the water and long for fish; go home and weave a net.

The man who removes a mountain begins by carrying away small stones.

Wednesday — *December 7*

DO you find choosing Christmas presents for other people difficult? Well, the preacher Lloyd John Ogilvie may have the perfect idea for you. It's the perfect thing for any occasion – and it's free!

"The secret of life," he wrote, "is that all we have and are is a gift of grace to be shared."

So, when you don't know what to give, give yourself!

HOLDING FAST

Thursday — **December 8**

WE are always being told to count our blessings but surely we ought to do more than just count them. Jeremy Taylor, who was known as "the Shakespeare of the divines" and was chaplain to King Charles the First, had this advice for those wondering what else to do with the gifts we have been given.

"The private and personal blessings we enjoy," he wrote, "deserve the thanksgiving of a whole life."

So count those blessings – then live a life that shows how much you appreciate them!

Friday — **December 9**

JOHN Bunyan once said, "You have not lived today until you have done something for someone who can never repay you."

Think about his words and see if you can lend a helping hand to someone in need – now!

Saturday — **December 10**

HERE is an excerpt from Naomi Shihab Nye's poem "Kindness" which gives great insight into this life-enhancing quality:

Before you know what kindness really is
You must lose things,
Feel the future dissolve in a moment
Like salt in a weakened broth,
What you held in your hand,
What you counted and carefully saved,
All this must go so you know
How desolate the landscape can be
Between the regions of kindness.

Sunday — *December 11*

PAUL Morphy, born in 1837, was probably the greatest chess player in the world during his lifetime. Legend has it a friend once took him to an art gallery and showed him a painting called "Checkmated".

It showed a distraught man staring at a chess board. He seemed to have lost the match. Even worse, his opponent was the Devil.

Paul studied the board for a while, then exclaimed, "I can still save him!" If a chess master would consider hundreds of moves to save a painted man, how many more ways do you think Jesus Christ would try to save you and me?

"For the Son of Man came to seek and to save that what was lost." (Luke 19:10)

Monday — *December 12*

LUCY wants to change the world. She is only fourteen years old yet dreams of some day living and working with orphaned children in Africa. She wants to help feed and clothe them and teach them how to read and write.

Sometimes well-intentioned friends and relatives try to discourage her from her ambitions; they'll suggest she might be happier staying at home and becoming a teacher or perhaps a social worker, but Lucy cannot be persuaded to change her mind.

Eleanor Roosevelt said, "The future belongs to those who believe in the beauty of their dreams," while Ferdinand Foch said, "The most powerful weapon on earth is the human soul on fire."

When we stand up for a cause with courage, our dreams can take us — and others — far.

Tuesday — *December 13*

TWENTY years ago Rose lost her sight, yet she has managed to maintain a surprising amount of independence.

She has mastered the art of simple cooking, can do some cleaning and light gardening and enjoys up to five audio books every week. One day, I asked her what her secret was and she replied:

"Helen Keller said the best and most beautiful things in this world cannot be seen or even heard, but must be felt with the heart. Since I lost my sight I reach out to experience life with my heart."

A wonderful way to live each day, surely.

Wednesday — *December 14*

PLATO said, "At the touch of love, everyone becomes a poet."

Now, there's a challenge to consider: how many people can you inspire today to create beautiful poetry?

Thursday — *December 15*

THE pleasure that comes from pottering in the garden or taking a walk along a leafy lane can be hard to describe. It's almost a physical communion with the natural world, touching and reviving the soul.

The Grand Old Man of Nature, essayist and naturalist John Burroughs said:

"One of the hardest lessons we have to learn in this life . . . is to see the divine, the celestial, the pure in the common, the near at hand — to see that heaven lies about us here in this world."

Friday — *December 16*

THERE'S nothing quite like the sight of a Christmas tree for putting the Lady of the House in a festive frame of mind. There's something special about the combination of lights and greenery, so I was interested to learn how the tradition is said to have started.

It seems it began in the 1530s, the inspiration of Martin Luther who translated the Bible into German. Riding home late one night, he was so touched by the beauty of the starlight shining through the forest branches that he decided to take a small tree home with him and decorate it with candles for his children to enjoy.

Within a few years, trees all over Germany were being decorated with crystallised fruits, apples, ginger and cinnamon, rolled wafers and sweets. Later this idea was popularised in Great Britain by the royal family.

A little starlight can create a huge amount of joy!

Saturday — *December 17*

OUR friend John loves his new hobby of painting and he also likes to donate the best of his work to charity. Ken just can't get enough of his three grandchildren's company and lively, non-stop chatter. Octogenarians Tom and Ellen walk hand in hand.

There are different kinds and degrees of love but all of us, just like my friends above, are better off for having it in our life, whatever kind it is.

As John Lennon said: "It matters not who you love, where you love, when you love or how you love. It only matters that you love!"

Sunday — *December 18*

HERE is a reading as Christmas approaches: "It was no Summer progress. A cold coming they had of it at this time of the year; just, the worst time of the year, to take a journey, and specially a long journey in. The ways deep, the weather sharp, the days short, the sun farthest off in *solstitio brumali*, the very dead of Winter."

This simple telling of the coming of Mary and Joseph to Bethlehem dates from 1622. The words are from Lancelot Andrewes, a famous preacher known as the "Angel of the Pulpit", and also the "Star of Preachers".

He was familiar with a total of fifteen languages and presided over the forty-seven scholars who were nominated by James I to work on the 1611 Authorized Version of the Bible.

Monday — *December 19*

IN December 1903 Orville and Wilbur Wright sent a telegram to their sister, Katharine. Greatly excited, she ran straight to the local newspaper and showed it to the editor. It read, "We have actually flown one hundred and twenty feet! Will be home for Christmas."

The editor, who knew the Wrights, replied, "How nice, the boys will be home for Christmas." Manned flight had just become a reality, but the editor looked at the message and failed to see its true importance.

As Christmas approaches let's enjoy the glitter and tinsel and parties, but let's not lose sight of the message behind it all — a miracle much greater than Orville and Wilbur's first flight!

Tuesday — **December 20**

HERE'S an unusual quote from an obscure historical figure. Georg Christoph Lichtenberg was an eighteenth-century physicist who once said, "Never undertake anything for which you would not have the courage to ask the blessing of Heaven."

I heard a mother express a similar sentiment to her son in a much more down-to-earth way.

"If you are wondering whether what you're about to do is right or wrong," she told him. "Imagine how you would feel explaining it to your grandmother."

Of course, there is no greater authority than Heaven — but grandmothers do come close!

Wednesday — **December 21**

LOOK for little pleasures, and the small, beautiful things in life. Treasure life's happy moments. Do not let them escape your notice. They are bright, golden threads in the cloth of life, and who would not agree with E. M. Forster, when he wrote:

"There is charm in little things."

Indeed there is — so start looking for them today.

Thursday — **December 22**

DURING the festive season when unusual presents often seem hard to come by, I find myself agreeing with these words from Burton Hillis.

"The best of all gifts around any Christmas tree: the presence of a happy family all wrapped up in each other."

Friday — *December 23*

HERE is a bouquet of thoughts for keen readers. The first one was found in a Victorian memoir by Lady Holland: "No furniture so charming as books."

Sir Richard Steele, essayist and playwright, wrote in "The Tatler" in 1710: "Reading is to the mind what exercise is to the body".

So many of us find that books are good companions — both new and old — and treasured friends on life's journey.

Saturday — *December 24*

THE audience is hushed and still,
The lights are dimming low,
A drum roll — and then curtain up,
It's time to start the show!
And here they come — the fairy queen,
The hero young and bold,
The heroine, all songs and smiles,
The goose, whose eggs are gold.
The dizzy dame, in dress bizarre,
Forever in a tizz,
The villain creeping up behind,
Oh no! "Oh, yes, he is!"
They strut across the gaudy stage,
On strange adventures bound,
Yet still we know that in the end
They'll all be safe and sound.
For this is an enchanted world,
Where tales are wove anew.
It's Christmastime, it's pantomime,
And every wish comes true!
                              Margaret Ingall.

Sunday — **December 25**

ROBERT STEVENSON, the grandfather of Robert Louis Stevenson, made his reputation building lighthouses on the most treacherous parts of the Scottish coastline, often living in the same accommodation and facing the same hardships as his men.

On the centenary of his birth a parade was arranged to celebrate his life. One of the banners bore the simple epitaph, *One Of Us.* It was a heartfelt message of acceptance and love.

When God wanted to touch the hearts of ordinary men and women he sent His son to become one of us:

"The Word became flesh and made His dwelling among us. We have seen His glory, the glory of the One and Only, who came from the Father, full of grace and truth." (John 1:14)

Monday — **December 26**

TOM ALGIE did not want to open his hardware shop on Boxing Day. He wanted instead to be at home with his family sharing precious time together.

But what about his customers? Well, he came up with a solution. He would, he decided, leave the shop door open and an honesty box behind the counter. That way he wasn't letting anyone down, he reckoned.

Next morning he found the box full. There were nearly two hundred pounds and several notes of thanks.

Wasn't that a heartening thing to happen at Christmastime?

SEASON'S GREETINGS

Tuesday — *December 27*

MANY years ago, it is said, a shepherd was stranded on Ben Alligin in Scotland during a snowstorm. Shivering, he huddled under an overhanging rock. Nodding off, he later opened his eyes to see a kilted Highlander standing over him, his beard encrusted with frost, his bare head white with snow. Only his eyes were warm.

Slowly, without a word, he raised his arm and beckoned to the shepherd. Forcing himself to his feet he followed the big man safely through the blizzard to the door of his croft, then his silent companion vanished. Nobody knew who he was.

A few years ago an English couple were climbing at this spot. A dense cloud of cold mist enveloped them and they could scarcely see their hands, let alone each other. They stayed still for a while but then they panicked, stumbling this way and that through the freezing mist.

Suddenly a figure, shaggy-maned and clad in old kilted plaid, loomed out of the mirk. In silence, he raised his arms as if to bar the way before the mist hid him again. The climbers shrank back, not daring to move an inch.

Seconds later, the cloud began to disperse; they saw that they were two feet from a precipice. They hurried safely off the hill and back to their hotel.

"Aye," said one local resident. "Angels don't always come with wings."

Wednesday — *December 28*

OUR doubts are traitors, and make us lose the good we oft might win, by fearing to attempt.   William Shakespeare.

Thursday — **December 29**

WHEN Brenda moved in to her new home she was delighted to receive several presents and greeting cards celebrating the occasion. But perhaps her favourite gift was sent by a friend who conveyed her good wishes in careful cross-stitch, using the words of preacher and poet Henry Van Dyke:

Every house where Love abides
And Friendship is a guest
Is surely home, and home-sweet-home
For there the heart can rest.

That message now has permanent pride of place upon her mantelpiece.

Friday — **December 30**

OUR friend Agnes saw this sign outside a church one day and it made her smile — and think:
Prayer — the best wireless connection.

I hope it brings a smile to your face, too, and gives you food for thought!

Saturday — **December 31**

OUR old friend Mary said that she used to wonder why people complained about time speeding by so fast — then as the years passed, she realised why! "Now it seems like the year has hardly started before it's over and a new one waits in the wings," she commented one day.

"The only bad news," said her neighbour Fred, "Is that time flies. The good news is that you are the pilot!"

Let's fly next year to somewhere worthwhile!

Photograph Locations and Photographers

MOUNTAIN HIGH — *Above Raven Craig, Moffat Hills.*
TRAVELLERS' REST — *Flam, Norway.*
CLEAR AS CRYSTAL — *Biddestone, Wiltshire.*
LET IN THE LIGHT — *St Mary's, Hartpury, Gloucestershire.*
THE GOLDEN PATH — *Cardoness Castle near Gatehouse of Fleet, Dumfries and Galloway.*
ON THE BEACH — *Killantringan Beach, near Portpatrick, Scotland.*
WILD AND WONDERFUL — *Bluebell Wood, Fryton, North Yorkshire.*
CROATIAN CALM — *Trsteno Harbour, Croatia.*
SUMMER SCENTS — *Priorwood Garden, Melrose, Scotland.*
BLUE HORIZON — *Portelet Bay and L'Ile Au Guerdain, Jersey.*
SUNNY SKETCHES — *Chania, Crete.*
GARDENER'S WORLD — *Anne Hathaway's Cottage, Shottery, Stratford upon Avon.*
FAITHFUL FOLLOWERS — *Ogmore Castle, near Bridgend, Wales.*
TRANQUIL TIMES — *Logan Botanic Garden, near Port Logan, Scotland.*
GLORIOUS GAUDI — *Sagrada Familia, Barcelona.*
SAFELY TAKEN IN — *Durisdeer, near the Lowther Hills, Scotland.*
SANCTUARY — *Monument To Loved Ones Lost At Sea, Kirkcudbright, Scotland.*
HOLDING FAST — *Gourock From Lyle Hill, Inverclyde, Scotland.*
SEASON'S GREETINGS — *Dundee, Scotland.*

ACKNOWLEDGEMENTS: **David Askham;** Clear As Crystal, Let In The Light, Are You Listening?, Croatian Calm, Sunny Sketches. **Ivan J. Belcher;** Gardener's World. **Paul Felix;** Now The Day Is Over, Faithful Followers, Poppy Day. **Douglas Laidlaw;** Travellers' Rest, Czech It Out! **Duncan I. McEwan;** Treasure In The Woods, Look Of Love, Tranquil Times, Holding Fast. **Rainer Walter Schmied;** Glorious Gaudi. **Willie Shand;** After The Rain, Summer Scents, Deep And Crisp, Season's Greetings. **South West Images;** Mountain High, The Golden Path, On The Beach, Safely Taken In, Sanctuary. **Sheila Taylor;** Perfect Partners, The Best Of Friends. **Richard J. Watson;** Wild And Wonderful. **Arch White**; In My Garden. **Andy Williams;** Blue Horizon.

Printed and Published by D. C. Thomson & Co., Ltd.,
185 Fleet Street, London EC4A 2HS.
© D. C. Thomson & Co., Ltd., 2010